THE PR
THE PEOPL_

A ROYAL PRIESTHOOD

Sotirios Christou

PHOENIX BOOKS

Unless otherwise stated Scripture quotations are from
The Revised Standard Version Cambridge Edition 1982

Cover by Penny Warden
Printed in Great Britain by
The Burlington Press Foxton Cambridge

We worship Jesus our great high priest
Who for the joy that was set before him
Endured the cross – despising the shame.

The way of Priesthood is the way of the cross
Embracing joy and suffering
Humiliation and glory.

In my faithfulness and in my failure
Lord have mercy – our great high priest.

Sotirios Christou

CONTENTS

CHAPTER ONE

PRIESTHOOD IN THE OLD TESTAMENT

CHRIST'S PRIESTHOOD IN THE NEW TESTAMENT

CHAPTER TWO

THE PRIEST AND THE PEOPLE OF GOD

CHAPTERS THREE – FIVE

THE PRIEST & THE PEOPLE OF GOD IN PARTNERSHIP

CHAPTER THREE

TRINITARIAN IMAGES OF PRIESTLY FORMATION

CHAPTER FOUR

TRADITIONAL IMAGES OF PRIESTLY FORMATION

CHAPTER FIVE

BIBLICAL IMAGES OF PRIESTLY FORMATION

CHAPTER SIX

'FORMATION – FORMATION – FORMATION!'

APPENDIX ONE

APPENDIX TWO

FOREWORD

I am pleased to write a foreword to this book on priesthood by my former colleague in ministry, Sotirios Christou.

There are many reasons at present why it is important to have a clear concept of priestly ministry. In recent decades, the Church has rightly seen the vital role in ministry of the laity. Lay people have been given an increasing role, and in some circles 'lay presidency' of the Eucharist is under discussion.

While the emancipation of the laity has been an unequivocal blessing in the life of the Church, it makes it all the more important to understand the nature of priesthood. We need to understand what priesthood is, how far it can be discharged by the whole body of the Church, how far it requires people specifically called to be priests and what the role of such people is. It is important for us to think theologically about such questions, as this book helps us to do, and not just see them as organizational issues.

Sotirios Christou has performed a valuable service by bringing together a broad array of Biblical and theological thinking about priesthood. Those who want to deepen and sharpen their thinking about priesthood will be hard put to find such a comprehensive introduction to the subject. I am pleased to recommend it to all concerned with this important topic in the life of the Church.

Fraser Watts
Senior Lecturer, Faculty of Divinity
University of Cambridge

PREFACE

In the middle of 2002, a friend was seeing the Diocesan Director of Ordinands, with a view to exploring his call to the ordained ministry. He was asked to read about being a priest and to lead a discussion with him on this topic during their subsequent meetings. I offered to lend him some books on this topic, and this fortuitous encounter led to the idea of writing a chapter on being a priest, in a book I was working on. The first half of this manuscript, "From The Pew To The Pulpit" was autobiographical, already over 30,000 words long and traced my Christian roots and pilgrimage in parish ministry, and was the context for sharing my vision for Pastoral Care & Formation Consultants.

As I thought about writing a chapter on being a priest, my instinctive reaction was to first look at the theology of priesthood in the Old Testament, as well as Christ's priesthood in the New Testament - which no contemporary book covers. This eventually became chapter one. Also as part of the background to being a priest, it seemed appropriate to refer to some of the current literature on this subject. This then became chapter two. However as my thinking on priesthood evolved this became chapters three to five and combined with my vision for Pastoral Care & Formation Consultants in chapter six - to contribute to training curates in the parish, it became increasingly obvious that I would have to reluctantly jettison my original manuscript and its autobiographical content; as writing on being a priest evolved into a book in its own right. Subsequently this book was written between January and May 2003 and the final draft was finished at the end of August.

As I continued to think about being a priest, I ruefully reflected that this was not a topic that was ever tackled when I was at theological college at St. John's in Nottingham. But now having had some time out from full-time ministry, due to the "roller coaster" impact of post viral fatique and having time on my hands, I thought further about the issue of priesthood. In hindsight I concluded that this a was a defining aspect of a minister's formation. However as an Evangelical I am aware that it is the Catholic wing of the Church of England, that is traditionally more established in preparing people as parish priests.

In one chapter in my original manuscript I was going to share my experience of post viral fatique. As this has been the immediate background to this book two paragraphs are given to briefly describe this illness. While there were times when I experienced a physical lack of energy my main symptoms were internal and unseen. Shortly after the doctor diagnosed this illness at the beginning of 98, during the month off she insisted I take, I had a picture that described my experience. It felt as if someone had drawn a circle around my emotional life and thrown it away, and also drawn another circle around my spiritual life and thrown that away too. My inner resources had been attacked, depleted and stolen. My inner life had been fragmented: and the wholeness and sense of well being I had before going to Sussex had evaporated. As a result there has been a prolonged and an acute sense of loss.

Despite this the irony is that on occasions I looked rather well. On returning to Cambridge to study for a year, at times in the first few months when I sat in the pew worshipping, there was literally a physical pain in my heart. Around this time when I also took the occasional 8 am Communion I had to force myself to do this, as I felt a strong reluctance not to. Consequently I knew within the first two to three years of this illness I did not have the inner resources to be involved in full time ministry.

This illness was punctuated by the disheartening and frustrating tendency of its fluctuating nature. There were regularly times when I felt that I was getting better, only to find that a negative downward turn would invariably follow. Despite the uplifting occasions it felt as if there was an internal negativity which had descended like a cloud and enveloped my heart and spirit. On a couple of occasions this caused me to question everything which I had been through, since the Lord called me to leave my secular career in 1978 to serve Him.

One of the most discouraging symptoms felt as if this endless roller coaster cycle of going up and then down was never going to end. On a handful of occasions as I went for a walk I remembered God's covenant love and clung on to it. At these particularly difficult times I reminded the Lord that ministry was His idea, that He started it all and He was responsible for sorting it out. A statement of trust and hope in the Lord. This has been a lonely pilgrimage with only the Lord really seeing and understanding what happened. Ultimately it has meant learning patience in a much more protracted way than I have ever known, and trusting that as Isaiah 53: 10 says of Christ, "it was the will of the Lord to bruise him....the will of the Lord shall prosper in His hands", and that on occasions this is true in our lives too.

During thirty nine years as a Christian, which includes fifteen as an ordained minister, I have observed many parish priests of different churchmanship, who after a number of years appeared to "stand still" in their ministry. I believe all of these ministers required ongoing training in their formation as parish priests. But as this officially ended after their first curacy they did not have a comprehensive enough formation to nurture this ongoing development. This is an important issue to address as a large number of ministers may never fulfill their potential. Consequently in chapter six I recommend that each diocese employ or designate suitable people as Pastoral Care & Formation Consultants, to contribute to the training of curates-priests in parish life and enable them to fulfill their potential, and continue growing and maturing in their priestly formation.

In the Diocese of Ely I have especially valued coming across priests from a Catholic background and churchmanship. To my pleasant surprise they were Biblical, Orthodox,had a deep faith and relationship with God and Christ and were secure in their faith. This was quite an eye opener to an Evangelical whose roots can be traced to All Souls Church, Langham Place W. 1. I will always be grateful for having learnt to celebrate Communion working with one such priest, the Rev. Dr. Fraser Watts. A clinical psychologist, a man of faith and spiritual depth, and a senior lecturer in the Faculty of Divinity at Cambridge University, for a number of years now. In All Saints Harston, one of the two churches we ministered in we wore vestments, which I adapted to fairly naturally, as I sensed that what mattered before the Lord was the disposition of one's heart and not what we were wearing.

During my time in the Diocese of Ely between 1992 – 1995 and 1998 – 2003 I have had an unusually formative experience, having been asked to preside (celebrate Communion) and preach in just over twenty different churches and also to celebrate the Eucharist at one theological college. The churchmanship of these parishes has varied from Catholic to Charismatic, to Evangelical and traditional. These parishes have included churches in Cambridge to rural ones and this has been a tremendous learning experience. I am now inclined to think that it should be a requirement in a curate's training, that at least once a month on a Sunday he/she helps out and worships in a parish whose churchmanship is different from their own. This would facilitate a more comprehensive formation for Anglican parish priests, as well as enable them to understand and sympathise with the broad spirituality of the Church of England.

My aim in writing is to explore the issue of priesthood for the priest and also for the people of God. Equally I hope this will encourage those training as ministers, to form a long term vision which can help to shape their priestly formation too. This exploration about priesthood is a pilgrimage which embraces many different phases. As both the priest and the people of God explore the images of priestly formation which I write about in chapters 3-5, I trust this will help them to form a creative partnership which animates and influences this journey together. A partnership which transcends a merely functional relationship, and which becomes one of relating to one another in their distinctive priestly calling and gifting.

The issue of the risen, ascended, glorified Christ as our great high priest tends to be a somewhat neglected subject, and yet one which I believe is close to the heart of God and central to understanding Christ's contemporary ministry.   Therefore I trust and pray that the priest as well as the people of God, find the relevance of Christ's priesthood in their lives to be breathtaking, inspirational and liberating - because it is all of these things. For me, one of the highlights, is the focus on the wonderful truths - about Jesus our great high priest.   R. C. Moberly says: "If we want to see in what the priesthood of the Church consists, or what the word priesthood ultimately means, we must first examine what it means in the Person of Christ".[1]

The issue of priesthood also integrally involves the Church, and in a generation which has rightly discovered the liberation of the gifts and ministries within the body of Christ, there is the danger that the identity and nature of the Church may be swallowed up by a focus on "ministry". As ABM Paper No 13 "Recovering Confidence – The Call To Ordained Ministry In A Changing World", perceptively points out:

> It is with the idea of priesthood that we encounter most directly the Church as a mystery, as being itself part of the revelation. The Church's rediscovery and affirmation of its own priestly nature is crucial to its search for identity. [2]

In search of this identity, we cannot help but focus on Christ's priestly sacrifice on the cross, which is the defining symbol of Christ's priesthood and which in turn is symbolic of the priestly nature of the Church. T. F. Torrance says:

> The form of priesthood in the Church derives from the form of Christ as the Suffering servant. [3]

He goes on to say:

> The conception of the Suffering servant is the great characteristic of the Church's ministry, and it is that which above all determines the nature of priesthood in the Church. [4]

These words were written nearly fifty years ago, and may well prove to be prophetic in the life of the Church in the 21st Century.

Sotirios Christou
Cambridge 2003

ACKNOWLEDGEMENTS

I am grateful to Ken and Judy Duke and Eva and Mandy Hanlon, who felt called to support me in prayer during this project when I wrote asking them to consider this. Their prayers have marked a noticeable turning point in the roller coaster impact of post viral fatigue.

I am grateful to the Revd. Lyndsay Meader for looking at the initial draft of what eventually evolved into chapter two. I am delighted to have made contact again with the Revd. Julian Charley who taught me on Sunday afternoons forty years ago, in the Jucos affiliated to The Covenanters, at All Souls Clubhouse London W. 1. I am grateful to him for having read through the initial draft of my manuscript, and for his suggestion to move my vision for Pastoral Care & Formation Consultants to the last chapter.

I am grateful to the Christian artist Penny Warden for giving me permission to use a picture she painted, for my front cover and which is part of The Phoenix Series. What I particularly like about this painting is that it contains a wealth of rich imagery. For me it captures something of the essence of Christ's priesthood. Although there is no cross in this painting, the cross nevertheless stands out and speaks to us about consecration and sacrifice: about being set apart for God and about the divine love and holiness of life which under girded this. Something which R. C. Moberly echoes when he describes the priesthood of Christ as, "an offering which is not more an outward enactment, than an inward perfecting of holiness and love."[5]

In this painting Christ is depicted as one who is suspended. There he speaks to us about offering one's life in serving God. This hints at a dynamic tension in being stretched to the limit perhaps even to breaking point, yet at the same time it reverberates with the possibility of hope and new life. The figure of Christ also portrays the risk of being vulnerable by being in other peoples' hands, and also captures the humiliating possibility of being seen to be helpless and weak. It also resonates with the theme of suffering, not necessarily physical, but emotional, mental and spiritual. But it also speaks movingly of the emergence of the power of God and of resurrection. In my imagination Penny's painting captures something of the essence and challenge of priesthood. A call to follow in the footsteps of Christ, not to an ecclesiastical office: and acts as a reminder to the priest and to the people of God, of Ashley Benedict's insight: "Christ is the model, the exemplar, the one from whom we learn what being priestly is all about."[6]

The Phoenix Series is an exhibition of paintings first seen at Holy Trinity, Guildford in 2000. Early Christian tradition adopted the Phoenix as the symbol of both immortality and resurrection. Penny's theology and a continued search for answers to the problem of suffering inspired The Phoenix Series. For more information about her work or possible commissions of the Phoenix paintings, she may be contacted at 9 Connaught Close, Crowthorne, Berkshire RG45 7QE. Telephone 01344 750346 EMail Address: www.pennywarden.moonfruit.com

I would like to express my appreciation to my father and mother in law, Lord and Lady Paulson. Without their support these past five years we would have floundered as a family with our twin boys, David and John. A glorious and joyful handful! I would also like to express my appreciation to my wife Sarah, who has borne her share of suffering as the wife of a priest. As the life of the priest is almost always in the hands of other people, her life has invariably been in the hands of other people too. As Christ served the Father he too placed himself in the hands of other people, as he set his face towards the cross. Yet Christ trusted that everything and everyone was ultimately in the sovereign hands of the Father. And from death came resurrection.

John Udris movingly shares from his experience that priesthood is placing oneself in God's hands in complete abandonment, something which as a control freak is a constant challenge to him. He shares that priesthood involves the struggle with his ongoing conversion to trust God with all his concerns, fears and weaknesses as he serves Him; and to learn to surrender the control of his life into His hands. He says, "In his abandonment prayer Ignatius prays, "You have given all to me, now I return it". I have to say I choke on that bit; but it's something Abraham could say and really mean."[7]

PRIESTHOOD IN THE OLD TESTAMENT

INTRODUCTION

Establishing the origin of priesthood in the Old Testament as well as examining the meaning of Christ's priesthood in the New Testament, is the context of the exploration concerning the formation of the priest, and the people of God as a royal priesthood. To consider the issue of priesthood in the Old Testament, inevitably involves taking into account the issue of sacrifice as they cannot be separated. In the Old Testament the office of a priest was primarily bound up with offering sacrifices on a daily basis, and this involved a diversity of sacrifices that God had instigated. For example there was the "burnt offering" in Leviticus 1, the "cereal offering" in Leviticus 2, the "peace offering" in Leviticus 3, the "sin – purification offering" in Leviticus 4 and the "reparation offering" in Leviticus 5. Equally sacrifices could not be offered up to God by anyone except the priest, who was called and ordained with the God given authority to do so. Reading through Exodus, Leviticus, Numbers and Deuteronomy may leave us with an antiquated feeling concerning the issue of priesthood and sacrifice, as these detailed instructions about the tabernacle and how various sacrifices offered up by the priests may now seem irrelevant and obsolete. However while we may not wish to get bogged down with the particular details about how the tabernacle was constructed or how the sacrifices were to be offered by priests, it is important to grasp some underlying truths which are relevant to exploring the issue of priesthood.

GOD GIVES THE GIFT OF PRIESTHOOD

The starting point for understanding the theology about priesthood and sacrifice in the Old Testament has to begin with God himself. Here it is important to remember that God took the initiative to instigate the priesthood and sacrificial system, after he delivered the Hebrews from bondage in Egypt and drew the people of Israel into a covenant relationship with himself; on the conditions he laid down in Leviticus 26: 14 – 46 and Deuteronomy 30: 1 – 20. This relationship instigated by God was a sign of His grace. God gave the tabernacle along with the priesthood and sacrificial system to His people and these too were all a sign of His grace. The Hebrews had done nothing to merit deliverance. God was setting them free from the Egyptians because of his promise to Abraham in Exodus 2:24: "And God heard their groaning and remembered his covenant with Abraham, with Isaac and with Jacob." Deliverance was solely on the grounds of God's grace. Priesthood in this context was supremely a gift by God to His people through His covenant promise. The tabernacle where the sacrifices could be carried out was also a gift to God's people, as it acted as a perpetual reminder of His presence with them. The sacrifices however were also a reminder of God's holiness and Israel's sin. Sacrifice as a gift enabled atonement for sin to take place as God had decreed. Therefore God could dwell in the tabernacle in the holy of holies in the midst of His people. As a result a covenant relationship could continue through the sacrificial system the priests carried out.

Concerning priesthood and sacrifice Gordon Wenham says, "at the heart of this scheme was the establishment of a pure system of worship, in which God could be honoured and praised in a fitting manner, and through which human sin could be atoned for."[1] This highlights for us another important aspect of the purpose of the tabernacle, priesthood and sacrifice. The offering to God of acceptable worship. Worship was the calling of the nation when God delivered them from Egypt, as we see from Exodus in 3: 18–19. Worship according to the instructions God was going to give to His people.

At the heart of priestly life as it evolved there was also the responsibility to teach God's people His Word and His ways. To provide them with spiritual guidance and to instruct the people concerning the Law, which would have included teaching the meaning of the Torah (as the Law in general was referred to). For example one aspect of Eli's responsibility as a priest was to judge Israel which he did for forty years (1 Samuel 4: 18). A role based on administering the Law of Moses. Then again in 2 Chronicles 17: 7 we learn that Jehosaphat commissioned princes, Levites and priests to go and teach the Law throughout all the cities of Judah. In Nehemiah we also see the important role of the priest in teaching the people from the Law and explaining the meaning of it to them. After the people had rebuilt the city walls and gates of Jerusalem, we learn from Nehemiah chapter 8: 1-8 that all the people gathered together and Ezra the priest read the Law of Moses to them the entire morning; and with the help of others explained the meaning of it to the people. The priestly role of teaching is also echoed in Malachi 2:7, "For the lips of a priest should guard knowledge and men should seek instruction from his mouth, for he is the messenger of the Lord of hosts." However one of the indictments made against the priests by the Lord in Jeremiah 2:8 was that they did not seek the Lord, and that those who handled the Law did not know Him.

GOD THE ARCHITECT
OF THE TABERNACLE AND WORSHIP

When we read the account of God giving Moses precise details about building the tabernacle and the altar, and instructions about the sacrificial system and the ordination of Aaron and his sons as priests; it is a salutary reminder about God's meticulous attention to detail about these things. It is a reminder that forgiveness – atonement, and a covenant relationship and worship were only possible because of God's initiative. While the nation was invited by God to contribute gifts in building the tabernacle (Exodus 25: 1-9), no initiative whatsoever is allowed by Him to be offered by Israel concerning the architecture of the tabernacle, the sacrificial system, choosing the priests, atonement, the covenant relationship, or worship. God looked for absolute obedience to all the detailed instructions He gave concerning all these matters: as God was the architect of both the tabernacle and Israel's worship.

These things were only possible on God's terms. Israel's obedience and trust was to be a sign of submission to God's sovereignty in these matters. It is illuminating to see from

Exodus chapter 32 where the people under Aaron's leadership make the golden calf and worship it, that they are still deeply influenced by the prevailing spirit of idolatry that has pervaded their stay in Egypt. Aaron goes along with the people in making the idol and they assume this is an acceptable way of worshipping the Lord and celebrating their deliverance. The people said in Exodus 32: 4 – 6, "These are your gods O Israel, who brought you up out of the land of Egypt! When Aaron saw this he built an altar before it; and Aaron made proclamation and said, "Tomorrow shall be a feast to the Lord." And they rose up early on the morrow and offered burnt offerings and brought peace offerings; and the people sat down to eat and drink and rose up to play." This incident is located in between God giving Moses in Exodus 19 – 32 the ten commandments, detailed instructions about building the ark of the Covenant and the tabernacle and instructions about the priests and various ordinances. This incident clearly illustrates the polluted and unacceptable worship God's people were in danger of offering to the Lord when acting on their own initiative. For as yet they did not understand the implications of their sin and God's holiness and that this could only be dealt with by God himself and on his terms, rather than by humanly instituted sacrifices that reflected the prevailing, sinful culture of their day. Moreover they did not understand that a relationship with God was also only possible because of his gracious activity, rather than by appeasing him with sacrifices they had initiated.

In contemporary society as we worship the Lord both the priest and the people of God as a royal priesthood have to take great care, especially when they seek to be contemporary and relevant in their worship, that they are not in fact capitulating

without realizing it to the prevailing spirits of our age.   What
God's people may deem acceptable and appropriate in their
contemporary worship, may in fact be counterfeit, idolatrous
and unacceptable to Him. It is important to prayerfully reflect
on the underlying truths, principles and purpose of the content
and style of our worship, and to carefully think through to what
extent God and Christ are both the object and subject of our
worship in all that we seek to do. To evaluate how acceptable
our worship is to the Lord and to be listening to Him, that He
might show us where any prevailing spirits of the age have
insidiously infiltrated it.

GOD THE INSTIGATOR
OF THE DAY OF ATONEMENT

As we think about priesthood it is important to mention
blood, as this was an integral feature of the sacrificial system.
An understanding of the significance of blood helps to clarify
the fact that sacrifices in the Old Testament, acted as a
typology for the sacrifice of Christ and the shedding of his
blood in the New Testament. G. Wenham reminds us, "under
the law almost everything is purified with blood and without
the shedding of blood there is no forgiveness of sins(Heb 9:
22)."[2]   In Leviticus the shedding of sacrificial blood is
regularly associated with cleansing and sanctification. "All
these sacrifices involved the shedding of blood and all these
sacrifices reached their annual climax, on the Day of
Atonement. On this day each part of the tabernacle was
smeared with blood."[3]

The Day of Atonement was a special day in the rhythm and routine of religious sacrifices in the life of Israel. Before the high priest offered a sacrifice for the sin of the nation, Aaron had to make a sin offering for himself and for his household and then the holy of holies itself had to be cleansed too. Aaron had to sacrifice a bull as a sin offering for himself and enter the holy of holies with a censer full of coals from the altar before the Lord, with two handfuls of incense beaten small and bring it within the veil and put the incense on the fire before the Lord; that the cloud of the incense may cover the mercy seat which is upon the testimony lest he die by being exposed to God's glory in the holy of holies. Then he had to take some of the blood of the bull and sprinkle it with his finger on the front of the mercy seat and before the mercy seat and sprinkle the blood with his finger seven times (Lexiticus 16:11-14).

Then Aaron had to kill the goat of the sin offering for the people and bring its blood within the veil and sprinkle its blood on the mercy seat and before the mercy seat. In this way he made atonement for the holy place because of the uncleanesses of the people of Israel, and because of their transgressions. He had to do the same for the tent of meeting. Then he had to cleanse the altar before the Lord, also with the blood of the bull and the goat by sprinkling it on the horns of the altar (Lexiticus 16:15-19).

When Aaron had finished making atonement for these things, he had to present a live goat in the holy of holies and lay both his hands on the head of the goat and cover over him all the sin of the people of Israel. Then he presented the goat to the people and sent him away into the wilderness, with a man ready to take

him there (Lexiticus 16:20-22).   The goat was symbolically
taking the sin of the nation away into the wilderness. A sign that
God had put away the sin of His people. Philip Jenson says, "the
particular emphasis of the sacrificial system and the priesthood
is that order, grading and hierarchy are central organizing
principles in the Levitical system. In this way the cult seeks to
integrate all aspects of Israel's life and bring them under God's
rule."[4]   He also points out, "'the tabernacle and its sacrificial
system is thus a gracious gift from God which allows a liberated
people to worship and serve God in holiness." [5]

AUTHENTIC PRIESTHOOD

   T. F. Torrance has some particularly perceptive insights about
priesthood in the Old Testament, which he sees as being in the
context of both God's covenant with Israel and the Word of God
to her. The importance of this background is a reminder that the
sacrifices and offerings made by the priests, did not have any
saving power in and of themselves. Their saving power came
from being a response to God's divine instructions, as all priestly
action could be traced to God's self revelation of Himself within
the covenant and in His Word (which He gave to Moses). This
shows that God was not merely responding to man's priestly
sacrifice, instead He was responding to the obedience of the
ordained priesthood He had instituted.[6] This was a sign of God's
gracious covenant activity rather than an elevation of this office.
In other words God and His character remained the central focus
of priesthood, rather than man and his priestly activity, for as
Torrance says, "it is actually God Himself who performs the act of

forgiveness and atonement, but the priestly cultus is designed to answer His act and bear witness to His cleansing of the sinner."[7]

Torrance also grasps a very profound issue concerning priesthood in the Old Testament, as he discerns Israel's attempt to change the sacrificial priesthood so that it stood by itself independently of God's Word; (which he sees as the story of Israel through the centuries). He justifies this by pointing out that the appeal of the worship of the nature gods and the feminine deities to Israel, represents the temptation to fashion worship according to man's desire; while the tendency to make the sacrificial priesthood independent of the prophetic Word of God, represents the temptation to escape from direct meeting or encounter with the living God.[8] In effect Israel sought to erect the divine ordinances of worship into priestly ritual so that it was efficacious (had a saving power) on its own. 'This was the great sin of Israel as she tried to make the Temple and its liturgy independent of God's Word and to assimilate it to the worship of nature....'[9]

Torrance also says, "against this independence and perversion of priesthood and priestly liturgy, God sent the prophets, most of them out of the priesthood itself, to protest against the transmutation of liturgy into idolatry, against the transmutation of liturgical forms of witness into hardened and self sufficient forms that only ministered to Israel's false security."[10] God's response to this is seen in some of His utterances through the prophets, for example in Amos 5: 21 the Lord says, "I hate, I despise your feasts and I take no delight in your solemn assemblies. Even though you offer me your burnt offerings and cereal offerings, I will not accept them: and the peace offerings of your fatted beasts, I will not look upon". A similar indictment of false security is made by God in Jeremiah 7: 4, "Do not trust in these deceptive words: "This is the temple of the Lord, the temple of the Lord, the temple of the Lord." As we read Jeremiah chapter seven we see the Lord was concerned with His people's behaviour when he says, "Will you steal, murder, commit adultery, swear falsely, burn incense to Baal and other gods, and then come and stand before me in this house which is called by my name and say, "We are delivered! – only to go on doing all these abominations?" Equally in Amos chapter five we see the Lord wanted his people to focus on matters of justice, mercy, obedience, righteousness and truth.

In effect Israel's priesthood, established within God's character revealed in the covenant and in God's will revealed in His Word, faced the possibility of being distorted and lacking integrity and acceptance in God's eyes. As a result this would no longer be an authentic priesthood, firmly founded upon God himself and keeping His covenant. This would lead to Israel having a false perception of her spiritual status, founded on her election as God's people. In turn this would lead to a false confidence in their relationship with God as His chosen people.

The hallmark of Israel's priesthood, was maintaining her covenant relationship with God, which reflected a fear of, and a reverence for the Lord. Ultimately for Israel the authenticity of her priesthood, was not all about outward rituals involving sacrifice and offerings. But the inner priestliness, of loving the Lord with her heart, soul, mind and strength.

CHRIST'S PRIESTHOOD IN THE NEW TESTAMENT

CHRIST'S COMPLETE PRIESTHOOD

The book of Hebrews is resplendent with priestly and sacrificial language concerning Christ. Here Christ is portrayed as our great high priest who has passed into the heavens (Heb: 4:14), a minister in the sanctuary and true tent which is set up not by man but by the Lord (Heb: 8:1-2). As we recall God taking the initiative and giving Moses detailed instructions about building the tabernacle and the ark, setting up the sacrificial system and appointing priests; here too we are reminded that Christ being appointed our great high priest in the heavenly sanctuary, is completely God's initiative too.

In this vividly symbolic book of scripture about Christ, the author compares the priesthood and sacrificial system in the Old Testament with Christ's priesthood and what he has achieved through his sacrificial death on the cross, as our great high priest. He clearly expounds some wonderful truths about Christ's complete priesthood in heaven, (complete in the sense that it is perfect and lacks nothing) which supercedes anything that the priests in the Old Testament were able to accomplish. As a result the people of God have been designated a royal priesthood, having inherited this title from Israel. Therefore it is of intrinsic value to the issue of priesthood to understand the accomplishment and significance of Christ's priesthood.

Raymond Brown succinctly highlights some aspects of Christ's complete priesthood. He see this as a victorious priesthood as Christ's offering of himself as a sacrifice for the sins of humanity is complete and does not have to be repeated, whereas in the Old Testament sacrifices for sins had to be constantly repeated.   He also sees three strands of truth connected to Christ's priesthood.[11] First Christ is our great high priest as his work far surpasses that of the Old Testament priests, and the accomplishment of his priesthood has made their sacrificial offerings obsolete.   Secondly Christ is also portrayed as a human priest. One who knows, understands and sympathizes with our weaknesses although he himself is perfect (Heb: 4: 15). Thirdly Christ is a unique priest as he is the Son of God, for united with Christ's humanity is his divinity.[12] There is also a fourth aspect of Christ's priesthood which he does not mention from this context in Heb 4: 14 -16, and that is that Christ's sacrifice as a priest was possible because he was sinless, which we see from verse 15. A reminder of the purity of sacrifice without blemish which had to be offered in the Old Testament.

CHRIST'S COMPASSIONATE PRIESTHOOD

The author of Hebrews also mentions Christ's compassionate priesthood and as we see from Heb: 4: 15 – 5: 4, this is a reminder that priests in the Old Testament had three qualifications. First they were called by God to act on behalf of men (Heb: 5: 1). Secondly a priest had to be sympathetic so he could deal gently with the ignorant and wayward, since he himself is beset with weakness (Heb 5:2). Thirdly being aware of his own sinfulness, the priest also offered up sacrifices for his own sins too. Christ's priesthood is compassionate because he fulfils these three indispensable requirements as a priest. So in Heb: 5:16 we are reminded, "We may come with confidence, to the throne of grace that we may receive mercy and help in time of need", because of Christ our great high priest, who compassionately represents us.

CHRIST'S SUBMISSIVE PRIESTHOOD

Hebrews 5: 4-8. speaks about Christ's submissive priesthood. This passage highlights that Christ did not presume to reach out for, grasp, or exalt himself to the status of high priest. Christ was called and appointed by God because of his godly reverence, his obedience and his sinlessness. His priesthood was rooted in his submissiveness as God's servant during his earthly life. We read in Heb: 5:8 about this submissive obedience, "Although he was a Son, he learned obedience through what he suffered."

The submission of Christ to the Father is a sublimely selfless quality, difficult for words to adequately describe. We might more readily appreciate this supreme attribute when we compare it to the competitiveness of human nature, often shown by people in selfishly enhancing their personal ambitions at the expense of others. Christ's submissiveness was a reflection of his love for the Father and for us, and also a sign of his willingness to let go of any personal ambition, to serve God and humanity.

CHRIST'S PERMANENT PRIESTHOOD

The readers of the book of Hebrews were Jewish Christians who were in danger of reverting to the Old Testament ceremonial rituals associated with Judaism, which explains the detailed exposition in Hebrews of priesthood in the Old Testament, in contrast to Christ's priesthood. The author has to be specific in referring to the priestly sacrificial system in the

Old Testament, in order to show that Christ's sacrifice as our great high priest, has put an end to this. As a result the author exhorts these Jewish Christians who were on the point of forsaking their commitment to Christ, to more fully hold onto their faith in him, by grasping how much more comprehensive, permanent and superlative Christ's priesthood is.

In Hebrews chapter seven we encounter Christ's permanent priesthood. In this Christ is likened to a priest after the order of Melchizedek and in verse 24 we read, "But Christ holds his priesthood permanently because he continues for ever." In fact the permanency of Christ's priesthood is introduced at the end of Hebrews 6: 19 –20 where we read, "We have this as a sure and steadfast anchor of the soul, a hope that enters into the inner :hind the curtain, where Jesus has gone as a forerunner :half, having become high priest for ever after the order :hizedek." It may be considered that this obscure e to Melchizedek could be overlooked, however it 1 integral part of the writer's presentation about Christ's ιod in contrast to that of the Old Testament priests.

y point in understanding the connection between Christ elchizedek, is to show that this contrasted sharply with wish priesthood, which was after the order of Aaron. The rstanding of Melchizedek's priesthood was that it was :ernal and effective, whereas Aaron's priesthood was temporary and imperfect and was now set aside by Christ, because of its weakness and because it was obsolete. Consequently Jesus is not a priest after the order of Aaron, but after the order of Melchizedek and therefore Christ's priesthood is permanent.

and the people of God. Whereas in the Old Testament only the high priest could come into the presence of God on behalf of all the people, once a year on the Day of Atonement, now everyone who trusts in what Christ's has accomplished by his death and shed blood, has priestly access into the very presence of God. Unlimited access into the heavenly sanctuary, into the very presence of God has been made possible by Jesus our great high priest: and drawing near to God and being in his presence, enjoying fellowship and communion with him is indeed a priestly privilege. It is much superior to anything the priests had access to or experienced in the Old Testament.

CHRIST'S COSMIC AND ETERNAL PRIESTHOOD

To fully appreciate Christ's cosmic and eternal priesthood it is helpful to look at the importance of Christ's blood from God's perspective, and consider what Christ offers to God in his contemporary ministry in heaven as our great high priest. Watchman Nee presents us with a profound insight concerning the shed blood of Christ, which is an integral part of his sacrifice as our great high priest. The blood of Christ is for our atonement, but forgiveness is not something the blood carries out on its own. The saving power of the blood of Christ is possible because of the value God places on it, and also because God has accepted it for the atonement of our sins.[14]   R. C. Moberly says something similar when he speaks of the culminating point of sacrifice in the Old Testament. This was not in the shedding of the blood, "But in the presentation before God in the holy place, of the blood that had been shed."[15]

Therefore Christ's ministry as our great high priest in the heavenly sanctuary prepared by God, is as Moberly points out, "Christ's eternal presentation of a life which eternally is the life that died. And in the life which Christ eternally presents to God, Calvary is eternally implied."[16] Ian Bradley focuses on the same theological truth when he says, "our Eucharist is the true representation of Christ's true and continuous sacrifice, once for all time offered on the earth - Golgotha and perpetually presented to the Father on our behalf in Eternity." He continues to say, "it is the eternal, sacrificial activity of the resurrected and ascended Christ and through him of God, with which the Eucharist links his body on earth."[17]

Bradley quotes one of Charles Wesley's eucharistic hymns which replete with sacrificial imagery make this point:

> Thou lamb that sufferest on the tree
> And in that dreadful mystery
>   Still offerest up thyself to God
> We cast us on thy sacrifice
> Wrapped in the sacred smoke arise
>   And covered with atoning blood.[18]

Bradley continues to quote T. Torrance about the Eastern liturgy:

> The eucharistic rite does not halt with participation in the body and blood of Christ (as in Western liturgies) but reaches into the self-offering of the risen and ascended Christ in his high priestly intercession before the face of the Father.[19]

As we read the book of Hebrews we glimpse the cosmic

significance of Christ's priesthood. In chapter 8: 1 we read,"….we have such a high priest, one who is seated at the right hand of the throne of the majesty in heaven", and we also read in chapter 10:12, "But when Christ had offered for all time a single sacrifice for sins, he sat down at the right hand of God." Christ who is seated in heaven at the right hand of God, exercises a cosmic priesthood because his ministry extends to the entire earth as well as to the heavenly places. His ministry as our great high priest transcends time and history and is eternal because of the accomplishment of his priesthood.

The cosmic impact of Christ's priesthood is also echoed in Ephesians 1: 9–10, "For he has made known to us in all wisdom the mystery of his will, according to his purpose which he set forth in Christ as a plan for the fullness of time, to unite all things in heaven and things on earth." Colossians 1: 19 –20 echoes a similar cosmic dimension, "For in Christ God was pleased to reconcile to himself all things, whether on earth or in heaven, making peace by the blood of Christ's cross."

The cosmic and eternal significance of what Christ our great high priest has accomplished by his death is breathtaking, for no longer does the sin of the priest and the people of God prevent them from approaching God and coming into His presence. No longer is it necessary for them to have a priest to represent them who comes once a year on the Day of Atonement into the very presence of God, because Christ has abolished the priestly sacrificial system in the Old Testament. Therefore the priest and the people of God have access into the very presence of God through Christ their great high priest. The truth of eternal access into God's presence is seen in

Heb: 10: 19-22, "Therefore brethren since we have confidence to enter the sanctuary by the blood of Jesus, by the new and living way which he opened for us through the curtain, that is through his flesh, and since we have a great priest over the house of God, let us draw near with a true heart in full assurance of faith, with our hearts sprinkled clean from an evil conscience and our bodies washed with pure water." This priestly gift of unprecedented cosmic and eternal access into the presence of God, would have been undreamt of by God's people in the Old Testament.

In considering the revolutionary truth that all of God's people have priestly access into the very presence of God, through Christ our great high priest, Paul in 1 Corinthians also presents us with another breathtaking truth. He says in 1 Cor: 3: 16, "Do you not know you are God's temple and that God's Spirit dwells in you?" He also says in 1 Cor: 6: 16-19, "Do you not know that your body is a temple of the Holy Spirit within you, which you have from God? You are not your own you were bought with a price. So glorify God in your body." The staggering truth is that God whose presence and glory dwelt in the holy of holies, now makes His home in the hearts of the priest and the people of God, who are described as a temple of the Holy Spirit. This is ground breaking truth, for through Christ our great high priest God lives in them, makes His home in them and manifests His presence in their hearts through the Holy Spirit. On the one hand they have priestly access into God's presence, and on the other hand as living temples, God's presence is now also within them.

Having received the gift of priestly access into the very presence of God and into the very sanctuary of heaven, Heb: 13: 15

reminds the priest and the people of God of their calling and privilege as God's holy nation and royal priesthood (1 Peter 2: 9); "Through Christ let us continually offer up a sacrifice of praise to God, that is the fruit of lips that acknowledge his name." Our priestly privilege in entering God's presence, is not only to interceed, but to also offer up worship that is the natural expression of hearts overflowing with thanksgiving, gratitude and praise for all that Christ our great high priest has accomplished for us. Worship that finds expression in Revelation 5: 9 -10 And they sang a new song saying:

> "Worthy art thou to take the scroll and to open its seals, for thou was slain and by your blood, didst ransom men for God, from every tribe and tongue and people and nation, and hast made them a kingdom and priests to our God, and they shall reign on earth".

Charitie De Chenez also captures this atmosphere of worship in a hymn she wrote, the first few lines of which are:

> Before the throne of God above
> I have a strong, a perfect plea:
> A great high priest whose name is love
> Who ever lives and pleads for me.
>
> My Name is graven on his hands
> My name is written on his heart.[20]

CHRIST'S JOYFUL PRIESTHOOD

In Hebrews 12: 2 we read, "Jesus the pioneer and perfecter of our faith who for the joy that was set before him endured the cross, despising the shame and is seated at the right hand of the throne of God." It is appropriate to end this chapter by focusing on the joy which Jesus our great high priest, anticipated and experienced. Having explored the different aspects of Christ's priesthood, we can readily grasp that his was a solemn choice to willing die an excruciating and humiliating death on the cross. Yet we can also glimpse that two aspects of Jesus' priesthood were a source of joy to him.

Firstly, although there is scant reference to Jesus' reactions to the healings and miracles he performed in the gospels, and a lack of feedback on his reactions to the individuals he encountered, we may readily imagine how much joy these occasions brought to him. Jesus would have experienced joy at seeing the kingdom of God having an impact in peoples' lives in these ways. He would also have known this joy when he saw people respond to him and his teaching about God as Father in the Kingdom of God. I imagine the crowds were often ecstatic with joy at the healings and miracles he performed, and I also suspect individuals reacted in the same way when they were healed or set free by a personal encounter with Christ. This joy is also reflected in John 15: 11 when Jesus said to his disciples, 'these things I have spoken to you, that my joy may be in you and that your joy may be full.'

Secondly, as Jesus discerned he was the "suffering servant" prophesied in Isaiah, Hebrews 12:2 allows us a glimpse into the joy he anticipated would result from the accomplishment of his sacrificial death. It is likely this joy embraced many things, such as the joy of our salvation. The joy of reconciliation between God and humanity. The joy of Jesus' anticipated resurrection. The joy of Jesus returning to the bosom of the Father in heaven. The joy of the giving of the Holy Spirit and the joy of the second coming. These were likely to have been some of the truths which inspired Jesus to be joyful.

The joy of Christ is something which Julian of Norwich expands on in "Showing of Love". Julian says:

> And with this our good Lord said blissfully, "Lo, how I love you."As if he had said, "My child, if you cannot look in my Godhead, see here. How I let open my side, and my heart is cloven in two and lets out blood and water, all that is in it, and this delights me and so will it delight you." "My darling, behold and see your Lord your God who is your Maker and your endless joy. See your own brother, your sovereign Saviour, my child behold. See what liking and bliss I have in your salvation. And for my love now joy with me."And also for more understanding this blessed word was said, "Lo, how I love you." As if he had said, "Behold and see that I loved you so much before I died for you, that I would die for you, and now I have died for you and suffered willfully that I may. And now is all my bitter pain and all my hard travail turned to endless joy and bliss to me. And to you For my delight is in your holiness and your endless joy and bliss to me. And to you."[21]

2

THE PRIEST AND THE
PEOPLE OF GOD

THE HISTORICAL BACKGROUND

It is both interesting and informative to trace the introduction of priests in the Church. Michael Ramsay, former Archbishop of Canterbury, succinctly sums up the development of Christian ministry, by pointing out in the second century came the distinction of bishop and presbyter and from this emerged the threefold ministry of bishop, presbyter and deacon. In the third century the title "priest" was first attached to bishops and subsequently to presbyters.[1] Michael Himes reminds us, "the presbyterate has its roots historically in the elders who governed the synagogue. This connection between the presbyteral office and the rabbinate helps to focus the priestly role today. As the rabbi's role is above all to be the guardian and interpreter of the Jewish tradition, so too the priest is the one who brings to bear the riches of the Christian community's tradition on the present life of the church, in order both to shape that life and enrich and expound the tradition."[2] The ordination rite even to this day speaks of presbyters and points to them having oversight of Christ's flock.

Steven Croft also informs us of the existence and role of presbyters in Jewish life. "The title presbyteros was extensively used in a variety of ways in Jewish scriptures, practice and the ancient world.....which means old and simply and literally means elder. Elders are found in Israel throughout the Old Testament from the Exodus onwards. They act as an informal group, as a kind of shared leadership, when the task becomes too much for one person.....Luke uses the term presbyteros to denote the corporate leadership of the Christian church in Jerusalem acting in council. The other place we find Christian presbyters in Acts is as a collective term to describe local leadership of the gentile churches, instituted by Paul and his companions. Leadership clearly influenced in some way by the pattern found in the Synagogues. The ministry of presbyters emerges from the Acts and the New Testament letters as the recognized and authoritative ministry of public and personal teaching."[3]

Presbyters for example are to be found in Acts 14: 21-23, Acts 15, Acts 20 and in 1 Timothy 4:14 and 5:15. David Power points out that in the early Church the bishop was the one who presided at the Eucharist. Presbyters were his companions and advisers who shared responsibility with him for church governance, while deacons looked to the needs of the poor. It was only when there were more communities than the bishop could serve that presbyters went to them to celebrate the Sunday Eucharist. Although teaching was also a key element in the presbyter-bishop's oversight of the life of the people: (Titus 1:9: 1 Timothy 5: 17).[4]

THE INSTITUTIONAL BACKGROUND

Bearing these developments in mind it is important to remember that the Church in its infancy was not recognized as an official institution. The Church was God's divine creation as the natural successor to Israel in the Old Testament. In its infancy the Church had to live alongside Judaism which was an officially recognized religious institution, but as there had been a degree of animosity between the Jewish religious leaders and Jesus the state would not recognize Christianity as an official religion. However by the third century Constantine changed all that when Christianity became the official religion of the state. K. Mason says, "Christian faith and worship came to take the place in society that older religious practices had taken, and Christian ministers came to be regarded as priests of that society."[5]

It is not surprising to find that some Christians have an institutional view of priesthood, seeing the priest in professional terms much as one would perceive a doctor or lawyer. People who provide a specific public service in a recognized role. In the same way the priest is seen as God's representative who performs some important religious roles, for example at funerals, weddings and baptisms. People in society look to priests at difficult times in their lives for assurance or about the search for meaning and purpose, and older, traditional church goers may also have a similar view of the priest. K. Mason says, "Priesthood receives its institutional character by way of the constant reiterated expectations that grow around it. With an official priesthood people know that they can expect certain things – even demand them, of members of the priesthood merely because they – the people are members."[6]

This view can prevent people from perceiving that priesthood is also the privilege of all the people of God. Such a stance may also see the priest as a privileged person set apart and superior to ordinary Christians. Still other Christians may feel somewhat resentful and not at all convinced about priests being "special", in the sense of being on an elevated spiritual level. They are right to question such a view for as we saw earlier in chapter one, in the Old Testament, priesthood is a gift from God and anyone called to be a priest in the institutional Church has this calling as a gift, and not as a reward for any achievement or merit.

THE SOCIOLOGICAL BACKGROUND

Bearing in mind the existence of the established Jewish religion, the newness of the Christian faith and the fact that in the early Church ministers are not referred to as priests, nowhere in the New Testament is there any indication that Christian priests would eventually serve the whole of society. However this is not surprising, as R. C. Moberly points out, "for the early Church to have used sacrificial and priestly language which was closely associated with the symbolic and ceremonial traditions of priesthood and sacrifice, integrally related to the temple, would have caused inextricable misunderstanding and confusion."[7] Only with the passage of time and the development of the theology of Christ's priesthood, could the concept of priest become more acceptable in the life of the Church.

Within three centuries after Christ's resurrection, Christian faith and worship came to take the place in society of older religious practices, and Christian ministers came to be regarded as priests of that same society. K. Mason observes, "the necessity of priesthood operates within all societies and primarily it is an articulation of social relationships in such a way, that the sacred becomes manifest through them. Moreover that although the whole church is priestly in a theological sense, it will still need its own peculiar priests in a sociological sense. This kind of priesthood understood as a social articulation, will be present wherever church life achieves some degree of social permanence. It will be present whether the word "priest" is used or not."[8]

Bearing in mind the existence of such a social priestly institution, we may well wonder how the institutional Church can more fully serve God in society? In contemporary society this involves the challenge to congregations, many which consist of older members, to wrestle in dialogue and prayer with the issue about passing on the inheritance of their faith to other people and often to a younger generation. Failure to fulfill this calling may well result in a progressive decline in church membership, with many churches becoming redundant in their communities.

The people of God also face the challenge of finding ways in their community to tangibly express their priestly vocation in terms of mission and service. This involves making contact with people in their parish to influence their awareness of the church, so that the community begins to understand the church's priestly dimension. This is important as the priesthood of all believers is not just a theological truth to bolster our self esteem. It is a dynamic term which may be interpreted in terms of outreach and mission, through the tangible priestly ministries of the people of God, of service and sacrifice in the community.

A SIGN OF PRIESTLY IDENTITY

One of the distinct expectations of the priest is that he/she is a symbol of the priestly identity of Christ, and is also a walking sacrament who personifies the characteristic priestliness of the Church. Kenneth Leech says, "To be a walking sacrament is to bear witness in one's body and life to the reality of God's grace…..the stress needs therefore to shift from that on skill and function to that on character and symbolic identity, to what R. C. Moberly called "The inwardness…of priesthood", which he saw as "The spirit of sacrifice."[9] This involves learning to daily die to self and sin and to rise to new life in Christ. The people of God are also called to this authentic inwardness of character.

The priest also has a representative priesthood and identity. Christopher Cocksworth quotes J. B. Lightfoot, "the minister is thus regarded as a priest because he is the mouthpiece, the representative of the priestly race."[10] The priest represents God and Christ to the church and the community and also represents them before God and Christ too. On the other hand the priest is also an example to the people of God of what it means to be a Christian, and this responsibility is not just a functional role which is relegated to a public relations act. The priest through a disciplined, prayerful communion with the Trinity brings God, Christ and the Spirit to others and is a bearer of the mystery of the Trinity. Being priestly means having access to God's presence, and being priestly is being in God's presence and involves representing the Church and the community before God and Christ. The people of God as a royal priesthood are called in the same way too.

A FUNCTIONAL OR SPIRITUAL PRIESTHOOD?

Over the years I have observed that one of the key issues in the life of the ordained minister, is the direction that is chosen which will influence his/her formation as a priest. This direction can probably be narrowed down to two choices. Is the priest going to become a functional minister, with ministry evolving around a predominantly practical emphasis on running an efficient church? Arthur Middleton believes this "reduces the roles of prayer and sacrament to a very low status."[11] Alternatively is the priest going to pursue an overtly spiritual direction which involves exploring the nature and formation of priesthood, so that all aspects of ministry including administration, flow from the deep spiritual foundations of prayer, the doctrines of Christ and the Church and is spirituality rooted in an authentic relationship with the Trinity? Ultimately what is at stake is whether the priest is going to capitulate to relegating ministry to a functional basis, which essentially supersedes the spiritual dimension of priesthood. While this may sound a rather blunt dichotomy, the priest has to choose what will determine and shape the many different aspects of parish ministry that he/she is involved in.

Arthur Middleton quotes Bishop Lightfoot's last charge to the clergy of Durham, in which he urged the "Yielding of ourselves up to the full influence of the Divine Presence" and "to endeavour to raise up in the hearts of their people such a sense of God, as shall be an habitual ready principle of reverence, love, gratitude, hope, trust…and obedience". Here the priest is seen as more than a mere functionary, but the one to whom is entrusted the spiritual guidance of the people in his/her charge.....the formation he/she gives them will be in accordance with the pattern of his/her own spiritual life."[12]

Kenneth Leech in writing about spirituality and priesthood highlights the importance of the priest being a person who can provide spiritual direction. He refers to Martin Thornton who saw this direction as the primary concern of the Christian priest or minister.[13] He also points out that Thornton related the loss of the understanding of priesthood to the prevalence of amateurism and incompetence in the things of the Spirit. He says, ..."I suspect that intelligent modern Christians are getting suspicious of clergy who are for ever engaged in something other than prayer....It is because a priest has time for prayer, study and reflection that his guidance of those in the world's hurly burly is likely to be worth having."[14]

R. C. Moberly also emphatically advocates the spiritual dimension of priesthood. He says, "the "inwardness" of a true priesthood requires the dedication of the inner life to Godward; of which again a necessary corollary is dedication of self on behalf of others."[15] He sees this as the "for otherness of priesthood" and says, "...the outward of administrative priestliness must be in perfect correspondence with the inward."[16] For the priest and the people of God this presents them with the challenge of ensuring that their outward priestly ministry and service, flows from an authentic inner spirituality rooted in the Trinity.

Ultimately this will determine whether theirs will be a functional priesthood that predominantly relies on spin-doctoring and maintaining an image through perpetual "spin", or whether it will be an authentic priesthood whose spirituality has depth and substance. To pursue the latter results in a priestly ministry which enables the priest and the people of God to mature spirituality. Whereas priesthood which relies pre-dominantly on "spin", lacks any real spiritual depth concerning the things of the Spirit.

THE HEART OF CHRIST'S PRIESTHOOD

The heart of Christ's priesthood embraced the union of his divine nature as God and his human nature as man. Therefore there is a fusion between Christ's divinity and our humanity which he took upon himself. The two characteristic qualities of this union, were the divine love of Christ which he lived out in a holy - sinless life on earth. It is this perfection of divine life lived in union with our humanity that enabled Christ to offer himself to God as a holy, sinless and perfect sacrifice. R. C. Moberly in effect says, the priesthood of Christ is the inward perfection of holiness and love, which made his sacrifice acceptable to God.[17]

Moberly contrasts priesthood in the Old Testament with Christ's priesthood and points out the former was merely outward and symbolic and enacted a sort of outward parable. As such it did not represent the essence of priesthood. However Christ's external sacrifice on the cross was an expression of his inward holiness and love, which culminated in his willing death.[18] In effect the heart of true priesthood embraces these things, in a life willing consecrated to God. For the priest and the people of God to reflect Christ's priesthood, involves embracing an inward priestliness, characterized by a spirit of holiness and love.

A PRIESTHOOD IN UNION WITH CHRIST

A.Middleton speaks of an ecclesial Christology which implies that Christ is not only to be worshipped but that he is also seen as a way along which we travel. In a nation characterized by a general decay of religion and an apathy and indifference towards the things of God, he sees that what is vital for the Church's witness and the challenge to the priest in contemporary society and the Church, is the fruit of a deeply lived experience of the mystery of Christ and this involves following the way of the cross in sacrifice and obedience in the concrete realities of living:

> A Church marked by the following of Christ, will be saved from the instinctive fear that meets every crisis by organizing itself into an administration, that wants to meet the difficulties by raising the organizational and structural level of the Church's resources.[19]

This train of thought also echoes that sooner or later a priest is faced with the choice of what is going to influence the direction of his/her formation. Will it be following Christ or the functional role of a priest, that steals Christ away from the people of God?

John Twisleton speaks about the priest as, "pointing people to Jesus and the intimacy he brings with God."[20] Michael Fallon similarly says, "the priest's experience, insights and decisions must be informed by his intimate communion with Christ."[21] It is clear that a pivotal influence in the formation of the life of the priest is determined by the direction he/she capitulates to. Will it be to the directional impulse and pull of the Holy Spirit to be formed and shaped in relationship with Christ, so that the people of God have a role model to emulate in their priestly formation; or is it to capitulate to a functional model whose aims are not spiritually rooted in a life deeply lived in communion with Christ?

THE PRIEST – ANIMATOR OF WORSHIP

It is the Holy Spirit who breathes life into the worship of the people of God. At the same time the priest is the one who can co-operate in this process of animation with the Holy Spirit in a number of ways. The priest can have excellent resource books on the subject, seek to understand the dynamics of both traditional and contemporary worship and occasionally experience different styles of churchmanship in worship too. He/she can also help the people of God about worship by teaching and preaching on this topic and encouraging them to learn about the subject themselves. The priest's central involvement in worship is all part of equipping the people of God, so they may be responsive to the animation of the Holy Spirit.

One of the integral aspects of the priest's role in worship lies in having been given the authority by the Church to pronounce absolution to God's People. In this way he/she is a sacramental sign of God's forgiveness through Christ to others. The priest also comes as a forgiven sinner to declare God's forgiveness to others, a declaration of Christ's grace which epitomizes the heart of the gospel. Through the Eucharist the priest is also a reassuring sign to the people of God of Christ's cleansing and absolution from their sins. Kenneth Stevenson, the Bishop of

Portsmouth, reminds us that the prayers of penitence are an essential ingredient of Communion. He says, "The confession of sin is regarded by many as the center of penitence but the gospel is about forgiveness, which means that the absolution, the declaration of forgiveness, puts the seal on this important preliminary. It is not about endless groveling. It is about a sober view of ourselves....It is in this spirit that we come to confess."[22]   Michael Perham says something similar.   "A prominent place for penitence has always been part of Anglicanism.....but in recent years there has been the tendency to play down this element....Penitence ought nearly always to be part of our approach to communion, but on occasions it should be brief and to the point, while on other occasions we should be prepared to give more time and space to this element of worship."[23]

The priest aims to be creative in leading the people of God in this act of penitence, through which the Holy Spirit can search their hearts and show them any hidden sins, or any presumptuous sins (Psalm 19: 12-13). M. Perham perceives, "....the burden of sin, even when we do not realize it, impairs our relationship with God and that no act of worship is complete without a recognition of that and a desire to put it right."[24]   He/she ensures there is a solid silence after the absolution, to allow this to have an impact on people's hearts and enable them to take in the precious balm of cleansing and forgiveness. Unless the priest enables the people of God in a meaningful way to clearly focus on the act of penitence, they may find the profound work of the Holy Spirit in renewal does not occur and instead they may have only flirted on a superficial level with this precious sacrament.

In thinking about the issue of penitence, the priest and the people of God might consider whether they are able to have a vicarious role in identifying with sin on a local, national and international level concerning the world and the Church. So that when local congregations come in penitence for their own sin they might also come penitently on behalf of others. This may well be a priestly ministry the people of God can exercise and for which we have a precedent in Daniel and in Nehemiah.

In chapter nine of the book of Daniel, he identifies with the sin of his people from the past even though he himself has not been part of it. He prays a prayer of penitence on their behalf by naming their specific and substantial sins before the Lord, pleading on God's character for mercy and forgiveness and for His wrath and anger to turn away; and for God's face to shine upon His sanctuary in Jerusalem and to do this for His own sake. Similarly in chapter one of the book of Nehemiah, he also identifies with the sin of his people and offers a prayer of penitence on their behalf. Such a prayer of corporate penitence on behalf of others releases God's forgiveness on events which those originally involved in, were probably never penitent for. This may well prevent the impact of other peoples' sin continuing to escalate.

This may be an opportunity for the priest and the people of God to interceed for local, national and international events and leaders in a powerful way, because God's people are now assuming responsibility on behalf of others. Such prayer prevents them from feeling helpless about events which they may be objectively distanced from. At the same time such prayer can in the long term release God's forgiveness and blessing on behalf of others, by invoking God's involvement in such matters; even though serious sins may have been committed and consequences occur. Penitent prayer on behalf of others may prevent the impact of sin being perpetuated for years on end, and may well be a priestly prerogative.

Whenever the priest presides at the Eucharist accompanied by the people of God, in their encounter with the risen, ascended and glorified Christ together they eagerly anticipate this symbolic act of rememberance, of mutual giving and receiving with the Trinity.   C. Cocksworth echoes this mutuality of giving and receiving when he speaks about the celebration of the Eucharist, "throughout the liturgy the unbounded self-giving of God to us allures us into the giving of ourselves to God."[25] As the life of the Trinity flows to us and through us, we in return are able to give thanks and praise, adoration and worship.

Scott Kahn reminds us that in the early Church the Christians baked the bread, pressed the wine for the Eucharist and also brought it forward at the offertory. He says, "the point is this, we offer ourselves and all that we have. Not because we are special, but because we know the Lord can take what is temporal and make it eternal, take what is human and make it divine."[26] Therefore the priest and the people of God as a royal priesthood, gathered together to celebrate Communion in the presence of the risen Christ, the Father and the Spirit may bring everything they have; themselves, their gifts, their failures, their ministries and symbolically lay them on the altar with the bread and wine which human hands have made. They come prepared to give because the Trinity graciously and unreservedly give themselves to the people of God in the Eucharist.

When the priest presides over the celebration of the Eucharist he/she is aware of the danger that liturgical worship can be dead and lifeless, unless it is saturated with prayer and animated by the Spirit. As the priest is caught up in worshipping the Lord and celebrates the Eucharist, in an attitude of prayer his/her soul is immersed in the truths which the Eucharistic prayer contains. J. Gledhill, The Bishop of Southampton, voices a similar sentiment, "to lead worship we must first be worshippers ourselves. Before Moses could be used as God's mouthpiece to Pharaoh and to his people, he was taken into the desert and saw the burning bush at Horeb. He could not have led his people to that mountain if he had not been there himself."[27] He also mentions the impact his first vicar had on him in the way in which he led worship. "You could tell that he himself had come fresh from the presence of God and was now going to lead us into that presence…..It sounds obvious but I learnt afresh that to lead worship you have to be a worshipper."[28]

Whenever I have led God's people in celebrating Communion I have always been struck by the impact of the timeless truths contained in the prayer of consecration and thanksgiving. After having been priested for some time I sensed an integration of the dual role of leading and worshipping at the Eucharist, and experienced a fusion between the prayer and myself which felt as if it had become an integral part of me. Accompanying this is an awareness of the anointing and empowering of the Holy Spirit which brings a sense of transcendence. This brings an awareness of being clothed in a tangible way with the Trinity. Kenneth Leech recalls that Thomas Merton reflects a similar experience, when he wrote of his sense, when celebrating the

Eucharist, of being taken out of his ordinary walking self into a different more authentic level of consciousness and personality:

> Day after day I am more and more aware that I
> am anything but my everyday self at the altar.[29]

This captures the sense of transcendence which the priest may experience when the Trinity flows through him/her in a heightened way, especially when celebrating Communion.

I have always felt it a tremendous privilege to celebrate Communion and when sharing this act of worship with God's people even in small rural congregations, I have known God's presence as my soul has been touched by the impact of the truths I am proclaiming. It is a mystery and also an experiential reality that through the priest and the prayer of consecration, Christ by his Spirit manifests himself amongst the people of God and touches their hearts and lives. And in the Eucharist through the symbols of bread and wine, the Holy Spirit transmits the eternal truth of the self giving sacrifice of Christ, to the people of God.

When a person is first priested as they celebrate communion they are concerned to get things right , so that the worship flows smoothly. As they are involved in the dynamics of worship, they are also concerned to be worshipping the Lord too, especially as they lead the people of God in worship which glorifies God. In seeking to ensure the Eucharist is spiritual rather than mechanical, the priest aims to be a person of prayer and worship in private. Through the discipline of attending to God in his/her devotional life, in turn this enables him/her to lead others in attending to God, in the sphere of public worship. C. Cocksworth quotes Robert Hovda's artistic description of leading worship; "and to preside is a function of unquestionable beauty and dignity", and then he profoundly adds himself: "good presiders "feel the freedom" of their role. They know their way around the liturgy. They feel the pulse of the people. They listen for the breath of God. They can move with the dynamics of worship giving space for spontaneity, room for silence and are trusted by their people to lead them towards moments of encounter with Christ, the head of the body."[30] Acquiring creativity, sensitivity and skill in leading the people of God in worship is learnt through the crucible of experience, through the study of worship, living a worshipful life and invoking the help and inspiration of the Holy Spirit. The temptation the priest has to be aware of is the danger of succumbing to a public performance, which distracts from worshipping the Lord and leading God's people in worship too.

One of the responsibilities of the priest is to teach and enable the people of God as a royal priesthood, to grow in their understanding and appreciation of worship and the Eucharist. I have been struck by the power of symbolism in the Eucharist which embraces so many central truths of the Christian faith, and which acts as a reminder to us of reconciliation, unity, peace, the kingdom of God, healing, liberation, forgiveness, Christian community, sacrifice, service, dying to sin and rising to new life in Christ and the second coming of Christ. It is possible to become so familiar with these things, that God's people may overlook the grace which can empower them to experience and live out these truths in their lives.

Here the priest can help the people of God by preaching on worship and the Eucharist, and by recommending books about these topics to the congregation which people can explore for themselves or in study groups. Despite these possibilities it is surprising how rare it is to receive preaching and teaching on these topics. I would go as far as to say this is an extraordinary omission, for the worshipping life of the Church can be enormously enriched when the priest teaches the people of God about worship. Douglas Dales in "Glory" the spiritual biography of Michael Ramsay, mentions a similar concern of the former archbishop concerning worship and the Eucharist when he says:

> ...The price too often paid was a familiarity with the sacrament and a shallowness of teaching, which destroyed the sense of reverence that he felt was appropriate and indispensable to eucharistic worship. Because Anglicans were 'at one in believing our Lord's sacrifice to be the great fact under whose shadow we worship',there should be more care in the way in which the sense and meaning of that sacrifice was taught. 'The awe in the individual's approach to holy Communion, which characterized both the Tractarians and the Evangelicals of old, stands in contrast to the ease with which our congregations come tripping to the altar week by week.'[31]

If a church's worship feels somewhat impoverished it may well be because of the lack of teaching and preaching on this topic. Consequently if the people of God are not enabled to grow in their understanding, experience and experimentation in worship, then it is likely that their corporate life will remain static and be shaped more by their cultural and church background than their priestly inheritance as the people of God. Yet potentially the ethos and identity of the people of God can be formed and transformed as a witnessing community through worship and the Eucharist. Douglas Dales mentions Michael Ramsay's insight about the transforming impact of the Eucharist:

> In the long run, the Eucharist will be its own interpreter and teacher. For the supreme question is not what we make of the Eucharist, but what the Eucharist is making of us, as together with the Word of God it fashions us into the way of Christ.[32]

A CREATIVE PARTNERSHIP

ACCM Occasional Paper 22 1987 states that the Church of England is committed to a "ministry of the whole people of God" and that within that to an "ordained ministry", and that each of these is seen as essential to the task of the church. Moreover these two kinds of ministries are bound to each other in proclaiming and realizing the creative activity of God in the world.[33] This report speaks of an inter-dependence and an inter-animative process between the priest and the people of God, which is reflected in a partnership between them. As an enabler the priest co-ordinates and releases the gifts of the people of God, and in turn they sustain and nurture the priest, therefore they animate each other..... and together they can do what neither alone can do[34]

There are powerful dynamic possibilities contained in this image of interdependence and inter-animation between the priest and the people of God, which can act as a catalyst for fulfilling the potential of their priestly calling. Learning to work in partnership in an essential factor in enabling this to happen. For the people of God as a royal priesthood this involves understanding the nature of their priesthood and its implications in the sight of God, because in His sight priesthood is not reserved for the select few who are ordained, but is the inheritance of all of God's baptized people.

R. Greenwood points us to the 1986 report, of the Church of England's Board for Mission and Unity's Faith and Order Advisory Group, "The Priesthood of the Ordained Ministry"-chaired by The Bishop of Chichester, Eric Kemp, in dialogue with contemporary ecumenical statements, which perpetuates the concept of the priesthood of Christ being mediated to the Church, through parallel but separate avenues of the whole baptized Church on the one hand and the ordained ministry on the other.

> The common priesthood of the community and the special priesthood of the ordained ministry are both derived from the priesthood of Christ. Bishops and presbyters do not participate to a greater degree in the priesthood of Christ: they participate in a different way not that is as individual believers, but in the exercise of their office.[35]

Integral to the partnership between the priest and people of God it is essential to have an enquiring heart and mind, so as they explore the meaning of being priestly their discoveries can influence their everyday lives and ministries to envision and transform them.

BEING PRIESTLY

Priests are God's gift to his Church to enable the whole people of God to more fully discover and appropriate their priesthood. They are also called to make Christ a present living reality to his people and through whom Christ manifests his priestly ministry. At the same time the people of God as a royal priesthood are God's gift to the priest and are also called to make Christ a present living reality within the Church and the community.

Christopher Gray a priest who was murdered in Liverpool in 1996, alludes to 1 Peter 2: 5 – 9 where the people of God are described as a "holy priesthood" and a "royal priesthood". He comments on these two texts, "they suggest that the whole Christian body is called to be priestly, a royal priesthood dependent on Christ.".[36] The concept of God's people as priests is an ancient image found in the book of Exodus 19: 6, "And you shall be to me a kingdom of priests and a holy nation". A reference to this ancient image is also found in Revelation 5: 10, "And thou has made them a kingdom and priests to our God."

C. Gray says, "any other sort of Christian priesthood if it is to be faithful to the New Testament, must fit in with the New Testament picture of Christ as the only true priest in the full sense of the term, and the whole Christian body being priestly in a secondary sense, dependent on Christ. It must be a particular ministry that is derived from Christ and promotes the priesthood of the whole body" and, "if one of the ways of being a Christian person is to be an ordained priest, that way of being will be priestly by not ursurping the priesthood of Christ, or of the whole body: but offering a likeness of the priesthood of Christ, in a life of sacrifice that makes Christ present and so helps the whole body to fulfill its vocation to be a royal priesthood."[37]

It is a timely reminder that from God's perspective being priestly means being able to come into His presence and being in an intimate relationship with Him. Whatever priestly ministries the priest and the people of God are involved in, or whatever priestly characteristic qualities they display, all these things flow from God's gracious initiative in their baptism into Christ's priesthood; through which they are designated a 'royal priesthood'.

> Ultimately, being priestly, flows from the privilege of being able to have access into God's presence: being in His presence and being in communion with God. And Christ our great high priest has made that possible.

We are reminded by R. C. Moberly :

> The ordained priests are priests only because it is the Church's prerogative to be priestly.....They have no greater right in the Sacraments than the laity: only they, and not the laity, have been authorized to stand before the congregation, and to represent the congregation in the ministerial enactment of the Sacraments...[38]

This reminds us that priesthood belongs to the whole people of God and is not the possession of the individual priest. As being a priest is an expression of this corporate identity, the minister's priesthood is one expression of the Church's ministries.

We may therefore ask whether the corporate identity of the priesthood of the people of God, should find expression in The Ordinal when deacons are priested? On this occasion the individual responsibility of the priest, could be firmly placed within the corporate responsibility of the people of God as a royal priesthood. We may also ask whether there might be an emphasis on the partnership between the priest and the people of God, which would alleviate the sole burden of responsibility placed on the person being priested?

THE PRIEST AND THE PEOPLE OF GOD IN PARTNERSHIP

INTRODUCTION

When a person is priested, The Ordinal (the service when deacons and priests are ordained) offers a series of images about priesthood which are explored in chapter four. Equally the Bible is full of images. We naturally use them in everyday life, and they can help to convey what it means to be priestly. The images of priesthood explored in the next three chapters can be used of Christ. Images not only paint a picture of being priestly, they can also symbolize what priests are called to be.

For the priest and the people of God as a royal priesthood there are many phases which they may go through in their partership and pilgrimage together. As the images of priesthood are incorporated into their formation, it is worth bearing in mind that some will continue in an ongoing manner throughout their life time. For example their formation in their relationship with God, Christ and the Holy Spirit are not one off phases they can pass through in a way which is final and complete.

TRINITARIAN IMAGES OF PRIESTLY FORMATION

I am aware that the headings - the image of grace, the image of reconciliation and the image of prayer in this chapter, may appear to be out of context. However they are included because they all flow from the initiative and activity of the Trinity.

THE IMAGE OF GRACE

The formation in grace of the priest and the people of God as a royal priesthood, seems to be the most suitable starting point in introducing these three chapters, as every area of priestly formation begins with God's grace, flows from His grace and is dependent on God's grace. It is also appropriate because no priest can be expected to grow in all these areas of formation on their own. Whereas the priest in partnership with the people of God can grow together in these ways.

An emphasis on grace also highlights the indispensable truth that every aspect of being a Christian in the lives of the priest and the people of God, begins with the initiative and activity of the Trinity. Whether it's their salvation or ongoing sanctification, their call to serve the Lord with the gifts He has given them, or whether it's their prayer life, worship, or any other aspect of Christian living; it is crucial to grasp that growth in any of these areas is not primarily dependent on them. Failure to grasp this foundational truth, results in a faith that relegates and transforms Christianity from a state of grace to that of law and good works. Once the priest and the people of God learn to put their trust in God's grace and rest secure in His initiative and activity, then they can have confidence to step out in faith and grow in the different areas of priestly formation.

Grace is one of the truths that the priest and the people of God are probably most familiar with, and by which the landscape of the Christian faith can be mapped out. Grace is a truth resplendent with meaning, embracing the heart of the gospel and God's gift of Salvation through Christ. Through grace we also receive God's overwhelming goodness and love towards us in Christ, which is completely unmerited by us. This is reflected in Ephesians 2: 7 – 9, "That in the coming ages God might show the immeasurable riches of his grace in kindness towards us in Christ Jesus. For by grace you have been saved through faith and this is not your own doing it is the gift of God – not because of works lest any man should boast." Grace also represents all of God's resources, His spiritual blessings and activity in our lives and also brings to us His sustaining and transforming power, and it is also a reminder of His unconditional love and acceptance.

In St. Paul we see an outrageous example of God's grace. Paul, formerly Saul, had plunged into the abyss of sinful self righteousness by persecuting Christians, and if anyone deserved judgment it was him. As he encountered Christ on the road to Damascus we see a classic example of God's generous grace to an undeserving sinner. After this he had an experiential reality and profound understanding of the full meaning and impact of grace, because he knew only too well that he was completely undeserving of it. Paul never ceased to be amazed at God's goodness towards him despite his fanatical persecution of Christians. We glimpse this in 1 Timothy 1: 13 – 14: ".....though I formerly blasphemed and persecuted and insulted him (Christ): but I received mercy because I had acted ignorantly in unbelief, and the grace of our Lord overflowed for me with the faith and love that are in Christ Jesus." Because of the abundance and the sufficiency and transforming power of God's grace, Paul would never be the same again.

The Lord seeks to lead His people into experiencing more of the resources of Christ's sustaining grace. We see such an example in the life of Paul in 2 Corinthians, when he prayed that the Lord would remove his thorn in the flesh. However in chapter 12 we see that the Lord does not always meet the needs of His people or answer their prayers in the ways they might choose. In verse 9 we see the Lord's reply, "But he said to me, "My grace is sufficient for you, for my power is made perfect in weakness." To which Paul's response was, "I will all the more gladly boast of my weaknesses, that the power of Christ may rest upon me." Paul was learning to rely on Christ's sustaining grace, even in his continual and painful weakness. Learning to rely on Christ's grace to meet our needs is a considerable challenge to God's people.

As a young Christian I was taught that the meaning of grace is "God's riches at Christ's expense". A definition anyone would find it difficult to improve on. George Herbert, Christian priest and poet, goes a long way in capturing the essence of grace in a poem he wrote.

> Love bade me welcome: yet my soul drew back
> Guilty of dust and sin.
> But quick-ey'd love, observing me grow slack
> From my first entrance in,
> Drew nearer to me, sweetly questioning,
> If I lacked anything.
>
> A guest I answer'd worthy to be here:
> Love said, You shall be he.
> I the unkind, ungrateful? Ah my dear,
> I cannot look on thee.
> Love took my hand, and smiling did reply,
> Who made the eyes but I?

> Truth Lord but I have marred them: let my shame
> > Go where it doth deserve.
> And know you not, says love, who bore the blame?
> > My dear, then I will serve.
> You must sit down says love, and taste my meat:
> > So I did sit and eat.[1]

Grace is God's bounteous provision for the priest and the people of God.

THE IMAGE OF KNOWING CHRIST

Christopher Gray says, "that priests are first Christians before they are priests."[2]   A priest is a Chrstian called to follow Christ and to be in a relationship with him, and the people of God as a royal priesthood are called in the same way too. So a priest is a Christian who follows Christ, is in a relationship with him and is also in the process of formation growing into the "likeness of Christ"and aiming to mature like him; and the people of God are called in the same way too. This process of formation includes growing in both the grace and knowledge of Christ and in practice this means getting to know and experience the many different facets of Christ's character, who he is and what he has accomplished as our great high priest. The people of God are called in the same way too.

Christopher Gray expresses the truth that the priest is called to grow up into the likeness of Christ, to resemble Christ and reflect the person of Christ in a particular way, for the sake of the body of Christ; as one particular image of Christ.[3] This aspect of what it is to be a priest is also clearly expressed in The Ordinal. In the declaration read before the actual ordination (page 357), those to priested are reminded that they are called to "grow up into the Lord's likeness." A priest is also called to reflect Christ's life of obedient sacrifice. The people of God have this same calling too. A priest is on a journey to discover the riches and depths of the friendship and Lordship of Christ and is also on a pilgrimage to increasingly discover and experience the love of Christ, with the help and inspiration of the Holy Spirit. The people of God are called in the same way too. A priest in seeking to learn more about and experience more of Christ, does not do so primarily for his/her own sake, but for the benefit of the people of God to share with them the unsearchable riches of Christ; that they too might comprehend and experience with "all the saints what is the width and length and depth and height of the love of Christ that surpasses knowledge, so that they may be filled with all the fullness of God" (Ephesians 3: 18–19). In turn the people of God as a royal priesthood may become a sacrament of God's love to the world.

A priest is a Christian who is nourished by the life of Christ and through whom the life of Christ flows by the power of the Holy Spirit. Christ is the vine and the priest is one branch. So a priest is a Christian who is constantly served by Christ and continually sustained by him (John 15: 1-7). A priest also points the people of God to Christ the true vine, that as branches joined to Christ they may be served and sustained by him and be fruitful in their priestly formation.

One of the things I have become aware of in recent years is of the necessity for all of God's people in their relationship with Christ, to have a profound encounter with him as their Saviour, friend and Lord. Without a profound experience of Christ in these areas it is extremely unlikely they will have a deep commitment to him. I believe this explains why so many youngsters and adults make a profession of faith in Christ, but do not continue to grow and mature in their commitment to him. The emphasis of Christ as Saviour is usually connected to a person's initial conversion or commitment to him, but I believe there should be an emphasis on the saving activity of Christ throughout the lives of the priest and the people of God.

There can also be an emphasis for the priest and the people of God to grow in their relationship with Christ by experiencing more of his friendship. The friendship of other Christians can reflect and symbolize the friendship of Christ too. As a young lad and then as a very young Christian teenager, one of the things that stood out in our leaders was that their transparent and uncomplicated love for us, reflected the friendship of Christ. Another way for the priest and the people of God to experience Christ's friendship is in their hearts, as they learn to follow him in their everyday lives. Two weeks after becoming a Christian and after returning home from our Christian camp, I clearly knew without a shadow of doubt that Christ was now with me and in my heart, as I responded to his love. From then on his friendship was as real to me as that of my closest friends; and I found great contentment and fulfillment in knowing Christ as a teenager and young adult.

For the priest and the people of God to grow in the formation of their relationship with Christ, also involves that they learn to submit to him as Lord of their lives. Through grace, prayer, and through the path of self denial – the way of the cross, and the ongoing commitment of every area of their lives, this can enable them to grow and mature in their relationship with Christ as Lord.

THE IMAGE OF KNOWING GOD

A priest is a Christian who is called to be in a relationship with God as Father, with the help and inspiration of the Spirit, and the people of God as a royal priesthood are called in the same way too.   Just as Jesus revealed God as Father to the first disciples through his life and ministry, through the Holy Spirit he continues to do the same for the priest and the people of God today in their priestly pilgrimage.   John 1: 18 shows us the sublime truth, "That no one has ever seen God. Jesus the only son who is in the bosom of the Father, he has made him known".   Jesus came to point people to the Father and he made the absolutely staggering claim in John 14: 9 "He who has seen me has seen the Father."

A priest is a Christian who is called to walk by faith in his/her relationship with God as Father and who is called to love God with his/her heart, soul mind and strength, with the help and inspiration of the Holy Spirit. A priest is also on a journey to discover the depths and riches of the character of God, and to experience His covenant love and activity in his/her life. The people of God are called in the same ways too. A priest is also called to point people to the Father through Christ and to reveal the Father's character.

It is sobering for all of God's people to realize that their intellectual knowledge of God, can easily overtake their experiential knowledge of Him.   This raises the danger of merely knowing about God as opposed to knowing Him personally in a relationship.   The priest and the people of God can guard against this danger by praying that their head knowledge about God becomes heart knowledge of Him. A descent from the head to the heart. For those whose spirituality is more naturally inclined to begin with the heart, the learning curve for them is to pray that their head knowledge of God increases and that in turn this also becomes a descent to the heart. Kenneth Leech reminds us what the 19th Century Bishop Theophan wrote about prayer: "the principal thing is to stand before God with the mind in the heart." This expression "the mind in the heart", is a favourite one of the Eastern Fathers and is their way of insisting that prayer must involve the unifying of the personality, the integration of mind and heart into one centre.[4] Knowing God is also a union of the heart and mind.

The priest and the people of God know, that knowing God begins with His initiative in calling them and drawing them to himself through Christ, through the work of His Holy Spirit in their lives. This initiative involves being pursued and taken hold of by God. Although of course they have the free will to resist his overtures of love, perhaps thinking in some foolish way they shall lose their freedom and pleasure. I still recall that moment in time forty years ago when God by his initiative spoke to me in my heart at the tender age of twelve, calling me to be a Christian and also giving me the desire to respond to Him. I was standing in front of the log fire at All Souls Clubhouse in Cleveland Street, (the youth club affiliated to All Souls Church Langham Place) in the West end of London, when I recognized God speak to me in the quietness of my heart. I instinctively knew the desire to be a Christian had come from God, as it was not something I had been thinking about. A theologically naïve young teenager simply knew with an inner certainty, uncomplicated by sophisticated adult logic, that God had spoken to him.

The priest and the people of God are aware that knowing God is not a one way relationship, in which they only get to know and understand Him. God calls them that He too might know them, individually and intimately in a personal relationship. Psalm 139 is a powerful testimony to the fact that God also knew David intimately and personally. In this Psalm the Holy Spirit reveals to David that God knew everything about him. He knew all that he did. He knew all that he thought. He knew all his personal traits which marked him out as a unique individual. David was deeply touched by the remarkable truth that God understood him completely and utterly. This "knowing" was enveloped with an element of mystery, which had begun even as he was being formed in his mother's womb. Just as we get to know a person by spending time with them, listening to them and understanding what matters to them and makes them tick, so too as the priest and the people of God spend time with God, listening to Him speaking to them through His word, they learn to understand more about His ways, His character and the things that matter to Him. As they do so they learn to delight in God and learn to love the things that He loves too.

It is a sign of maturity as the priest and the people of God grow in their relationship with God that they see beyond Him merely providing their needs, and are apprehended by the truth that there is something more sublime that helps to form and transform their walk with Him. It is the realization that this relationship is ultimately to glorify God, as they live to "the praise of his glory"(Ephesians 1:12). Undeniably at times this involves the way of the cross, the way of self denial, which seeks to put the interests and glory of God before their own.

As a teenage Christian and young adult my relationship with Christ was particularly real to me and I found great fulfillment in his love and friendship. However as a Christian in my early twenties, I then became increasingly aware of being drawn into a deep relationship with God as my Father. I began to sense more of the intimacy of his abiding presence in my heart and life too. In the autumn of 1981 I reflected on the changes that God had brought about in my life, and thought of the friendships that had been left behind and the tremendous sense of belonging they had once given me. I was inspired to write very simply about the intimacy of God's love and friendship and this is what I wrote.

> I Love you. Though you are unseen –
> Yet you dwell inside my being.
> Exactly what does my love mean to you?
> Yet it's what you are seeking.
>
> You've become the intimacy
> My soul has constantly yearned for.
> Through all my life's changes I see
> You're more to me than I had before.

The sentiments of a prayer of St. Thomas Aquinas 1225 – 1274 is a suitable one for the priest and the people of God to aspire to in their relationship with God.

> Give us O Lord a steadfast heart - which no unworthy affection may drag downwards.
> Give us an unconquered heart - which no tribulation can wear out.

Give us an upright heart - which no unworthy purpose
may tempt aside.
Bestow upon us also O Lord - understanding to know you
Diligence to seek you - wisdom to find you
And a faithfulness that may finally embrace you -
through Jesus Christ our Lord. Amen.

THE IMAGE OF KNOWING THE SPIRIT

A priest is a Christian, who is called to be in a relationship with
the Holy Spirit, with his help and inspiration, and the people of
God as a royal priesthood are called in the same way too.   The
Spirit delights to point the priest and the people of God, to both
the Father and to Christ. Tom Smail underlines that, "the primary
work of the Spirit is not connected to charismatic manifestations,
but with our initiation into the two central relationships that are
summed up in the two confessions, "Abba, Father" and "Jesus is
Kurios, Lord."[5]   The Holy Spirit is also the self effacing person
of the Trinity who does not draw attention to himself. Jesus
taught his disciples in John 16: 13b –14 "Whatever the Spirit
hears he will speak and he will declare to you the things that are
to come. The Spirit will glorify me for he will take what is mine
and declare it to you." This highlights what F. D. Bruner says,
"The ministry of the Spirit is Christocentricity."[6]

For both the priest and the people of God, it is important to
highlight that the Holy Spirit is the promise of the Father and a
gift to His people. Whatever their churchmanship may be the
Spirit is freely available and freely given to all of God's baptized
people. While some Christians may have experienced more of

the Holy Spirit in their lives, others may feel their experience of the Spirit is not as pronounced, and they have missed out in some way. However all of God's people, all have the same Spirit to receive and they all can grow in their understanding of the Spirit and in their relationship with him. F. D. Bruner says, "as the opening sentence in Acts unites the Holy Spirit with the work of Jesus, so the opening paragraph clothes the Holy Spirit with his proper name: the promise. The Holy Spirit is even at the very beginning Jesus' way of working in his Church (Acts 1: 1-2) and the Church will receive him freely, inclusively and indicatively – as a promise (Acts 1: 4-5)."[7]

Charles Stanley mentions some of the aspects of the work of the Holy Spirit in our lives: "The Holy Spirit convicts – John 16: 8-11. The Spirit illuminates – John 16: 12-15. The Spirit teaches – John 16: 12-15. The Spirit guides – Romans 8: 14. The Spirit assures – Romans 8: 16. The Spirit intercedes – Romans 8; 26. The Spirit directs – Acts 20: 22. The Spirit warns – Acts 20:23".[8] Of course the Holy Spirit can also be grieved as we see in Ephesians 4: 25-31. It is a simple but profound lesson that God does not call the priest and the people of God, to serve him in their own strength and natural ability. He has given the gift of the Holy Spirit to equip and help them in their priestly formation, and they are exhorted in Ephesians 5: 18 "To continually be filled with the Spirit".

At certain times in their lives the priest and the people of God may find that they are at different stages in their relationship with God, Christ and the Holy Spirit, and it's possible they may have progressed further in their relationship with God as Father than they have with Christ as Lord. Although of course it may be the other way round. Alternatively they may feel that they are making progress in their relationship with God and Christ, but they have not progressed as much in their relationship with the Holy Spirit. It is a timely reminder that it is God Father, Son and Holy Spirit who take the initiative in deepening their relationship with them, and being aware which of these relationships there is room to grow in, is a positive step in their relational formation with the Trinity. At times the priest and the people of God may find they relate to any one of the three persons of the Trinity, more in a functional role rather than in a relational way, which in practice means they relate to them more for what they do rather than in their personal relationship with them. When they become aware of this happening in any of their relationships with the Trinity, in prayer they can ask for the help of the Holy Spirit, so that this particular relationship may be deepened.

When a person is ordained deacon or priest, in the ordination service there is a specific emphasis on asking for the help of the Holy Spirit, and when the bishop addresses those to be ordained he reminds them, "...pray earnestly for God's Holy Spirit. Pray that he will each day enlarge and enlighten your understanding of the Scriptures, so that you may grow stronger and more mature in your ministry...(The Ordinal page 372)." And of course the congregation sing the hymn "Veni Creator" a moving and salutary reminder of their reliance upon the Holy Spirit, for the ministry of the priest and the people of God, would be impossible without Him:

Come Holy Ghost our souls inspire
And lighten with celestial fire;
Thou the anointing Spirit art
Who dost thy sevenfold gifts impart.

Thy blessed unction from above
Is comfort, life and fire of love;
Enable with perpetual light
The dullness of our blinded sight.

Anoint and cheer our soiled face
With the abundance of thy grace;
Keep far our foes, give peace at home
Where thou art guide no ill can come.

Teach us to know the Father, Son
And thee of both, to be but One;
That through the ages all along
This may be our endless song:

Praise to thy eternal merit,
Father, Son and Holy Spirit.

THE IMAGE OF TRINITARIAN QUALITIES

As a priest grows in his/her relationship with God, Christ and the Holy Spirit, this process of formation will affect and influence his/her relationships with the people of God, by reflecting the characteristic qualities of the Trinity. Therefore a priest in his relational formation for example, aims to mirror in his/her inter-personal relationship with the people of God and in the community, qualities of compassion, faithfulness, forgiveness, holiness, justice, mercy, reconciliation, righteousness, steadfast love and unity. The people of God as a royal priesthood are called to reflect these relational qualities too.

So the way a priest relates to the people of God and to those in the community will be influenced by his/her deepening relationship with God, Christ and the Holy Spirit. In this context the priest sets the people of God an example to deepen their corporate relationship with the Trinity, as well as their individual relationships with one another too. Therefore a priest is supremely a Christian involved in relationships on both a divine and human level. However the question is whether a priest's relational formation will reflect the relational qualities of the Trinity, or whether this will be influenced by and founded on his/her own ego, spin doctoring and worldly qualities. Ephesians 4: 29 – 31 warns against the possibility of Christians grieving the Holy Spirit in their relationships with one another by saying, "Let no evil talk come out of your mouths, but only such as is good for edifying, as fits the occasion, that it may impart grace to those who hear. And do not grieve the Holy Spirit of God, in whom you were sealed for the day of redemption. Let all bitterness and wrath and anger and clamor and slander be put away from you, with all malice." These worldly characteristics are to be superseded by the relational characteristics of the Trinity in the lives of the priest and the people of God, and lived out in their inter personal relationships.

Therefore authentic Christian community mirrors in the inter personal relationships amongst Christians, the relational qualities found within the Trinity. Such a community accurately reflecting these Trinitarian qualities, is an authentic reflection of relational life within the Kingdom of God here on earth. As the priest and the people of God seek to grow in this way, there is the temptation to think that these things can be accomplished in their own ability and strength. However just as the Trinity take the initiative to draw us into a relationship with them, so too the relational formation of the priest and the people of God is dependent on the initiative and activity of the Trinity.

THE IMAGE OF RECONCILIATION

The priest and the people of God are called to be involved in the ministry of reconciliation. This ministry is expressed in 2 Corinthians 5: 5: 18 – 19.

> All this is from God who through Christ reconciled us to himself and gave us the ministry of reconciliation; that is in Christ God was reconciling the world to himself, not counting their trespasses against them, and entrusting to us the message of reconciliation.

This is often a neglected ministry and a lost jewel of the Church's priestly calling. Yet the priest can set an example by educating the people of God, of the potential of this ministry which empowered by the Spirit they can exercise in their local community.

In an attempt to understand what reconciliation means within the heart of the Trinity, Miroslav Volf has some particularly profound and challenging insights about this area of formation. In talking about reconciliation as "embrace" he speaks about the cross and the centrality of forgiveness. He quotes Dietrich Bonhoeffer who clearly saw forgiveness itself as a form of suffering:

> That when I forgive I have not only suffered a violation, but surpressed the rightful claims of a restitutive justice.[9]

Volf points out that Christ's stance on the cross is not to let humanity remain an enemy, but creates space in himself for the enemy to come in. The cross says, despite humanity's vast enmity towards God, we still belong to God and the cross is a symbol of God's desire to break the power of human enmity without violence; and to receive human beings into divine communion – reconciliation.[10] He sees the divine initiative and willingness to embrace the enemy on and through the cross as undoubtedly a scandal, for the cross offers us outstretched arms. A naked body with a pierced side. Christ is the victim who has refused to be defined by the perpetrator, who forgives and makes space in himself for the enemy.[11]

When the Trinity turns towards the world, the Son and the Spirit become in Irenaeus's beautiful image, the two arms of God by which humanity was made and taken into God's embrace and that when God sets out to embrace the enemy, the result is the cross.[12]

As this vision of reconciliation is offered he visualizes on the cross the dance of self giving of the Trinity and the embrace of the enemy - humanity.

In the agony of the passion the movement of the dance stops for a brief moment and a fissure occurs, so that sinful humanity can join in. We the enemies – are embraced by the divine persons, who love us with the very same love with which they love each other and therefore so make space for us in their own eternal embrace.[13]

Volf roots this inclusive embrace of reconciliation for humanity, as now being inseparably joined to the Trinity in the Eucharist. This ritual time when we celebrate this divine "making-space-for-us-and-inviting-us-in." He believes we would profoundly misunderstand the Eucharist if we thought of it only as a sacrament of God's embrace, of which we are merely recipients. Instead written on the very heart of God's grace is the rule that what happens to us must be done by us, and therefore having been embraced by God we must make space for others in ourselves and invite them in, even our enemies. This is what we enact when we celebrate the Eucharist.[14]

This process of formation for the priest and the people of God into ministers of reconciliation, flows from the grace of God and is a gift of the Trinity. For most people reconciliation goes against their natural tendency for revenge, and too often Christians have attitudes and prejudices which exclude rather than include others. Wound rather than heal. Separate rather than reconcile. The first step in growing as ministers of reconciliation, is the revelation by the Trinity of our own need of reconciliation with God and with one another. For we cannot be ministers of reconciliation amongst the people of God and within the local community, when on a deeper level our hearts, minds and aspirations may have been malformed and need transforming into the likeness of Christ once again.

The cost of reconciling humanity into the very heart of God involved the embrace of the cross by Christ. It may be that at times for the priest and the people of God to be ministers of reconciliation, will be costly and involve suffering too. To embrace others in the name of Christ in an act of reconciliation, may not always be in freshly laundered garments, but in the soiled linen of everyday living. Nevertheless the joy of being reconciled to the Trinity and others, is indeed at the heart of the gospel and at the heart of being a eucharistic community. The challenge to the priest and the people of God is how to share the good news of reconciliation with the local community, that Jesus our great high priest waits to receive them with outstretched arms. A patient longing, and a loving waiting, to embrace those who are excluded. The challenge to be ministers of reconciliation is to have open and inclusive hearts, that have been transformed by the Trinity to embrace and make space for others. An authentic expression of eucharistic reconciliation.

The inescapable starting point for being such a community, is to learn to pray from the heart the Jesus prayer in this way.

> Lord Jesus Christ, Son of God have mercy on us sinners.
> Lord Jesus Christ, Son of God have mercy on me a sinner.
> Lord Jesus Christ, Son of God have mercy on us sinners.

THE IMAGE OF PRAYER

The overwhelming privilege which we clearly saw from the exploration of Christ's Priesthood, is that all the people of God have priestly access into God's presence and this is especially true concerning prayer. At times some of God's people may feel they have been called to a special ministry of intercession. However there is no elitism or superiority when it comes to prayer, for God's desire is for all his people to mature in their formation in prayer.

As a Christian I have always experienced a strong impulse and inclination to be prayerful which I believe emanates from God. However my initial understanding of prayer was limited to the aspect of intercession which was all that we had been taught. In time the Lord led me on a journey to discover the different melodies and movements that prayer embraces and I came to realize that the gift and mystery of prayer does not initially spring from or depend upon our expertise or eloquence, or even our particular method of praying. I believe the heart of authentic prayer originates from the heart of God the Father, who places into our hearts by His Spirit the desire of prayer, to draw us into a deeper relationship with Him and Christ so that we may learn to enjoy fellowship and communion with them.

I am convinced that God's delight and desire is for the priest and the people of God as a royal priesthood, to learn to enjoy spending time with Him and Christ in prayer.

It is liberating to realise that we do not have to approach prayer with a burdensome intercessory shopping list, but we can come with anticipation and delight into God's presence to primarily be with God and Christ. For we come to be with them for themselves.   Rosalind Brown echoes this truth when she says, "prayer then is the intimacy of our life with God. Prayer is being lost in wonder, love and praise."[15] Prayer is not initially about asking God and Christ for things, important though our requests may be. Prayer is coming to be with God and Christ for themselves. Coming to be with them for who they are is the starting point of prayer. I remember one particularly special period in my life in the early 1990's when I had no day time colleagues in ministry. I began each day, six days a week by coming into the presence of the Lord in prayer. I still clearly recall how much I looked forward to and delighted in coming into the Lord's presence. I eagerly anticipated being with the Lord, as the presence of God and Christ was so immensely satisfying. Their presence gave me a sense of wholeness and well being. Devoting time to them in this way was a joy to me and I trust also a joy to them.

Over the years as the Lord has taught me more about the different melodies and movements in prayer, this has helped to shape my rhythm and pattern of prayer. One of the things which gives me confidence in prayer, is to come by faith into God's presence through Christ, with the help and inspiration of the Holy Spirit. For me this has become a liturgical prayer as

I know that I can come into the very presence of God, into the holy of holies, because of what Christ by his death on the cross has accomplished. And I always ask for the help and inspiration of the Spirit to express my reliance on God in prayer. It is reassuring to know God gives His people the desire to pray: Christ makes it possible for them to come to God in prayer and the Spirit helps them in their prayer. For prayer is primarily a Trinitarian initiative and activity. The Lord looks to His people to be responsive and to give Him their attention, time and love. Kenneth Leech reminds us, "the Eastern Fathers insist that prayer is primarily the action of God."[16]

For the priest and the people of God in their busy lives their formation in prayer is a different type of work. It is the activity of the soul turned towards God and Christ, which acknowledges that any lasting spiritual effectiveness and impact as we serve them has to be rooted in prayer, otherwise what we do merely depends on us. Once we have tasted of the Lord's goodness in and through prayer, we find that coming to give ourselves to God and Christ is none other than our response to their overture of love. There is a giving and a receiving, which begins with God and Christ, flows to us and then returns to them: as we come to fix our gaze on them and their attributes. E. Underhill says, "We must receive before we can transmit, but sometimes we are in such a hurry to transmit that we forget the primary need to receive."[17] She also speaks of our activity in serving the Lord being first nourished by our adoration, so that the latter feeds the former. "The full Christian life of prayer swings to and fro between adoration and action. Be sure your outward swing to God is full, generous, unhurried, brimming with joy......If we can acquire the determination that nothing shall turn us from a steady, daily habit of adoration, our prayer will be full of loving awe and intimacy."[18]

In recent years I have used the shorter form of Morning Prayer as the foundation of my prayer time. Not only are the canticles in this rooted in scripture but there are also three scripture readings for the day, which provide solid content and which enable us to focus on the Lord. I have found this scriptural content is the basis of offering the Lord praise and thanksgiving. In 1977 the Lord showed me that the way of coming into his presence through Christ, was by praise and thanksgiving. Coming with a willing heart to offer our praise and adoration to the Lord can be quite uplifting. On those days when things are troubling my heart and mind, I take time to offer them up to the Lord and wait until he brings me his peace and stillness before continuing in prayer.

M. Ramsay, the former Archbishop of Canterbury, has some helpful insights about prayer and intercession. He says:

> We are called near to Jesus and with Jesus and in
> Jesus to be with God with the people on our heart.[19]

Or again about prayer he says, "but try to think of it more simply: it means putting yourself near God, with God in a time of quietness each day."[20] He continues to say, "the daily time of quietly being with God becomes "adoration". And because you are with him and near him whose name is love, you will have the people you care for on your heart."[21]

M. Ramsay's simple, yet profound picture, of being with God with the people on our hearts, points us to the way of intercession. As we surrender our ability to know what the right requests may be, and what peoples' deeper underlying needs involved in these requests are, we can come near to God and be with Him with the people on our hearts, in silent supplication or audible intercession. As we quietly and confidently bring people and situations to the Lord, we can bathe them in His love and care and we can hold onto the fact that God is trustworthy, so that we can come with the people on our hearts and leave them safely in His hands.

4

TRADITIONAL IMAGES OF PRIESTLY FORMATION

IMAGES FROM THE ORDINAL

At no time during my theological training at St. John's College, nor at the retreat leading to my priesting, was there any particular focus on what our formation as priests involved. Perhaps it was assumed that prospective priests are already familiar with this. In exploring the issue of priesthood for both the priest and the people of God as a royal priesthood, The Ordinal when deacons are priested contains a wealth of rich imagery, which if explored, can provide a good foundation for their formation.

When candidates to be priested are presented to the bishop, the charge which he reads to them covers a number of areas of formation (The Ordinal page 371-372). The various aspects of a priest's formation and ministry described in this charge, all involve areas of leadership and these areas have certain common factors. The priest is to be a trustworthy person who has been given authority by the Church to serve Christ and God's people. The priest is accountable to God and has oversight of Christ's flock which is a great responsibility. The priest's leadership is to be characterized by sacrifice, wholeheartedness and obedience to Christ and also by the qualities of being thankful and joyful, having Christ the Good Shepherd as their example (The Ordinal page 371).

While the rich imagery of the different facets of the priest's leadership, and the qualities described in The Ordinal can help shape his/her formation, it is prudent to balance this with two important insights. First God calls the priest into partnership with the Trinity to share in their ministry, as ultimately the overall responsibility and oversight of the Church rests firmly in their hands. This reminder helps to prevent the greatness of the peoples' expectations from becoming a burden to their minister. Secondly the people of God in partnership with the priest, can also share many of the same areas of priestly responsibility too.

As an integral part of the introduction to the traditional images of priestly formation, it is instructive to look at the importance R. C. Moberly places on the qualities of priesthood which The Ordinal focuses on. He places great emphasis on the inner quality of priesthood, which in effect he refers to as the inward dimension. He points out that gradually the Anglican Ordinal departed from placing a mere emphasis on the sacrificial nature of priesthood, which finds expression in celebrating the Eucharist. He goes on to say, "the formal celebration of the Eucharist may be the ......most glorious of its executive privileges: yet priesthood is something far more vitally inclusive...."[1]

He expounds the fact that the New Testament supremely advocates the inward character of priesthood. He says:

> It is the care of an utterly loving pastor, a shepherd who tends, feeds, nurses, rescues and is ready to die for his flock. All this belongs exactly to the that inner reality

of the spirit and life which......should be the true
inwardness of the outward representation of the
sacrifice of Christ.[2]

This is founded on the example of Christ as the good shepherd
who lays down his life for the sheep in John 10: 11. Moberly
continues to state that a spiritual inwardness of the office of
Church leadership as a whole, stands in the forefront of The
Anglican Ordinal which has restored what had been gradually
lost in the mediaeval Ordinal. What has been restored is:

The true proportion between the outward and the inward:
it has restored the essential relation and harmony
between Eucharistic leadership....and a right conception
in Christ's Church of the meaning of ministerial priesthood.[3]

He also says, "that true priestliness necessarily carries with it
the pastoral character: the real pastoral character is but an
expression, in outward life, of priestliness."[4]   It is this pastoral
character of being priestly which The Ordinal highlights as a
central aspect of a person's ordination to the priesthood.

THE IMAGE OF STEWARD

In the Old Testament as well as in the New Testament a steward
held an important and prominent position. He would have been
in charge of his master's household. This would have involved
authority, responsibility and also a position of great trust. The
term steward which was contemporary in Jesus' day was also
loaded with significance. However today the word steward

sounds somewhat antiquated and is obsolete in its original meaning, as we use it to convey something quite different. In Genesis 39: 4 we learn that Joseph found favour because his master Potiphar saw that the Lord was with him. Subsequently he made him overseer of his house and put him in charge of all that he had. As overseer his role was equivalent to that of a steward.

In 1 Corinthians 4: 1 Paul spoke about his ministry in terms of being "a steward of the mysteries of God". The priest as a steward faces the double responsibility of having leadership over the household of God, as well as having responsibility for the doctrine which the Church espouses. The formation of the priest as a steward also demands the quality of faithfulness in being in charge of God's household. These responsibilities which are shared by other lay leaders amongst the people of God, enable them to fulfill their ministry as a royal priesthood too. This area of formation also seriously takes into account that ultimately as stewards, they are accountable to God for the way they perform these tasks.

THE IMAGE OF WATCHMAN

In both the Old and New Testaments a watchman had a very responsible position. It would have been readily understood that his role was to act on behalf of a city, by keeping a lookout for any danger from invading armies and to sound the alarm when the enemy was spotted. The modern equivalent would be that of the sentry. A watchman had to be alert and vigilant keeping a lookout for any danger from his watchtower. A lonely and an isolated task and one which had to be performed day and night. Any failure to spot the approaching enemy through negligence of any sort may well have risked the lives of the inhabitants of the city. So the watchman was required to be absolutely faithful and trustworthy in carrying out his duty. In the Old Testament watchmen are mentioned as early on as in 1 and 2 Samuel and 2 Kings, then in Isaiah and Jeremiah.   The Lord specifically called Ezekiel to be a watchman. We read in Ezekiel 3: 17-19:

> Son of man I have made you a watchman for the house of Israel: whenever you hear a word from my mouth, you shall give them warning from me. If I say to the wicked, 'You shall surely die' and you give him no warning, nor speak to warn the wicked from his wicked way, in order to save his life, that wicked man shall die in his iniquity; but his blood I will require at your hands. But if you warn the wicked and he does not turn from his wickedness, or from his wicked way, he shall die in his iniquity; but you will have saved your life.

The striking thing about Ezekiel's call to be a watchman, is that the Lord was using this term in a new and unique way. Ezekiel's warnings did not concern Israel's enemies but warnings from the Lord himself. He had to warn Israel of God's words and communicate the Lord's intentions to His people. This was a great responsibility for Ezekiel which required him to be faithful in his duty as a watchman, as undoubtedly the messages from the Lord were not going to make him popular. However the solemn nature of his calling is indicated by the fact the Lord will hold Ezekiel responsible for the death of the wicked, if he does not give them the warnings from the Lord.   From Ezekiel 3: 17-19 we see that he was not only called to be a watchman for Israel, in effect he was also a watchman for his own life too.

The formation of the priest and the people of God as watchmen, requires courage, as such a task is not always likely to prove popular. The charge by the bishop at the priest's ordination, calls him to "admonish" and "to search for God's children in the wilderness of this world's temptations" (The Ordinal page 372). To admonish suggests to discipline. To warn people of what is wrong in their lives. Temptations suggests warning God's people of the danger of sin, as well as seeking our those who may have succumbed to such temptation. The priest and the people of God as watchmen, have the welfare of God's people on their hearts and are accountable to the Lord for their protection and well being. As such admonishing and warning are not authoritarian edicts, but reflect God's concern for His people. As watchmen they also admonish and warn with compassion and understanding. Even though they may feel this is a solemn task, they are ministers of God's grace, not His condemnation.

The priest and the people of God as watchmen also warn God's people of the wiles and ways of the evil one, of his deceit and lies and seek to highlight the ways in which they have been assimilated into our contemporary culture and church life. Their role as watchmen can also be a prophetic one with regards to addressing the Church, their local community or the nation.

THE IMAGE OF MESSENGER

In the Old Testament there are innumerable references to messengers, therefore Jesus' contemporaries would have been familiar with this term. A messenger might have a number of tasks to carry our for his master. He might simply have a message to convey as in I Samuel 2: 5. Equally the messenger would carry out his master's instructions as in 1 Chronicles 19: 2. Or he would make enquiries on behalf of his master, as John's disciples did when he sent them as messenger to ask Jesus if he was the Christ. Equally the messenger could be sent to get things ready or to prepare the way for his master's arrival. In Luke 7: 18-23 Jesus affirms to John the Baptist's messengers that he is indeed the Christ. John's arrival on the scene as God's messenger prophesied in Isaiah 40, would have been of great significance and a sign of assurance and confirmation to Jesus, that it was God's timing for him to begin his ministry.

The messenger in Jesus' day was someone who acted on the instructions of his master as he was under his authority. It would have been required of him to be reliable and trustworthy. Moreover he may well have been an influential person with a great deal of responsibility in his master's household, even though he was still a servant. As such he was accountable to his master. Although we tend to think more of Jesus as a servant he was also God's messenger, bringing the message of good news of the arrival of the kingdom of God. Jesus himself understood the inauguration of his ministry in these terms. We see this in Luke 4: 18-19 and 21, which is a fulfillment of Isaiah 61: 1-4.

> The Spirit of the Lord is upon me, because he has
> anointed me to preach good news to the poor. He has
> sent me to proclaim release to the captives and
> recovering of sight to the blind, to set at liberty those
> who are oppressed, to proclaim the acceptable year of
> the Lord. And he began to say to them, "Today this
> scripture has been fulfilled in your hearing."

The steward, the watchman and the messenger all have some
common characteristics. They were all under the authority and
instructions of their master and were accountable to him. They
were also required to be faithful, responsible and trustworthy.
The priest as a messenger also acts under God's authority and
is accountable to the Lord. He/she can be seen as a messenger
whenever the opportunity to preach or teach arises, speaking on
behalf of the Lord. Equally the priest can be a messenger in the
sense of an ambassador, acting on behalf of the Lord and
representing the Church. The people of God as a royal
priesthood can also be messengers in the same ways too.

THE IMAGE OF SHEPHERD

The bishop exhorts those who are being priested that "he/she
must set the good shepherd always before them as the pattern of
their calling, caring for the people committed to their charge (The
Ordinal page 371-372)." Equally part of the bishop's charge to the
priests is, "to feed and to provide for the Lord's family, to search
for his children in the wilderness of this world's temptations (page
372)." Tidball reminds us that Thomas Oden described the image
of shepherd as the "pivotal analogy" of ministry.[5]

The term shepherd was a very familiar one especially in the Old Testament as this was fundamental to Israel's pastoral economy. Even king David was once himself a shepherd. However in Jesus' day the image associated with shepherds had radically altered. It was definitely not viewed with the sentimental Christmas image we have of shepherds coming to see the baby Jesus. In Christ's day shepherds were seen as irreputable characters. Derek Tidball points out, "shepherds were considered to be constitutionally dishonest and had acquired a dubious reputation. People were not allowed to buy anything from them as it would probably have been stolen. They were listed among those who practiced a despised trade. Shepherds were stigmatized."[6]

We are readily familiar with Jesus' words in John 10: 1-18 where he speaks of being,"The good shepherd that lays down his life for the sheep." However I suspect we are not so familiar with the negative perception of the shepherd's image that had evolved in Jesus' day. It is against this background that Jesus speaks of himself as the good shepherd, identifying himself with the messianic claim to be the true shepherd of Israel, as is described in the very moving passage in Ezekiel 34: 11-12 and 15-16:

> For thus says the Lord God: Behold I, I myself will search out for my sheep and will seek them out. As a shepherd seeks out his flock when some of his sheep have been scattered abroad, so will I seek out my sheep; and I will rescue them from all places where they have been scattered on a day of clouds and thick darkness. I myself will be the shepherd of my sheep and I will make them lie down, says the Lord God.

I will seek the lost and I will bring back the strayed, and
I will bind up the crippled and I will strengthen the
weak, and the fat and the strong I will watch over.
I will feed them in justice.

Jesus fulfills the prophecy of Ezekiel 34: 11-16 that God
himself would shepherd His people. This was set against the
background of Ezekiel condemning the failure of Israel's
shepherds in caring for God's people. The shepherds are
accused not only of negligence but also of killing God's people,
"The weak you have not strengthened, the sick you have not
healed, the crippled you have not bound up, the strayed you
have not brought back, the lost you have not sought" (Ezekiel
34:4). Tidball says, "they had instead, ruled brutally. As a
result the flock had been scattered and destroyed."[7]   However
in John 10 Jesus speaks of himself as the good shepherd, in
contrast to the thief and robber who enter the sheepfold by
another way. Jesus is the good shepherd who knows his flock
personally by name (John 10:3). There is a personal
relationship between him and the flock and they know his voice
(John 10:4). Also he lays down his life for the sheep (John
10:11 and 10:15). Jesus the good shepherd proved to be faithful
and trustworthy even unto death, in contrast to the shepherds of
Israel.

It goes without saying that pastoral care is not the exclusive
concern of Christians. There are many secular caring agencies
in the community that provide pastoral care and support for
people. These can include volunteers as well as highly trained
and qualified professional staff. Christopher Seville says, "the
pastoral care of the Church is often compared with that of other

professional support agencies. Although parallels can be drawn there exists the important distinction that pastoral care within the body of Christ has a primary concern with the spiritual, as well as the physical welfare of an individual.".[8] Frank Wright describes Christian pastoral care by quoting two American authors, Clebsch and Jaekle. They define pastoral care as, "helping acts, done by representative Christian persons, directed towards the healing, sustaining, guiding and reconciling of troubled persons, whose troubles arise in the context of ultimate meanings and concerns."[9]

At the heart of Christian pastoral care is the heart of God and Christ. A heart that longs to help people find freedom and wholeness even through their troubles. Freedom as C. Seville says, "to find their 'real selves' and experience the abundant life that Christ promises he can bring."[10] Pastoral care takes place amongst the people of God as a royal priesthood and this invariably involves other Christians, and contributes to the growth and maturity of the Church. This enables us to not fall into the danger of identifying pastoral care as something for particular individuals in isolation. Moreover those who are involved in caring whether it is the priest or the people of God, also bring other divine relationships into the pastoral dimension. For they embody through their presence the heart of God, the love of Christ and the comfort of the Holy Spirit.

The priest and the people of God prayerfully exercise this pastoral priestly ministry. Their main aim is to point people to God, Father, Son and Holy Spirit. The ultimate source of all healing and wholeness. At times, pastoral care as Christopher Seville reminds us, may involve sharing Christ's love with people "through simple acts of service."[11] Often the priest and the people of God by giving their time, interest and concern for others give to them a listening heart, which represents the heart of God. As they listen they bring to them the precious oil of understanding. As they understand and stand alongside people through their troubles, they do not necessarily bringing slick and ready made solutions. Instead they also listen to the heart of the Trinity, seeking to bring their wisdom which will facilitate freedom and wholeness in the person's pilgrimage.

In some churches the people of God a royal priesthood are already well established in their pastoral formation as shepherds. Within this context the priest can be growing in his/her pastoral formation as a shepherd, by providing pastoral care for all the lay leaders too. That does not mean only supporting them when they have a problem or particular need. The priest can also provide pastoral care for these leaders on a regular basis by developing meaningful relationships with them. Within this context of regular care, trust is established and the priest cares for the strong leaders as well as those who are not so self reliant. This is the model that Jesus himself the good shepherd fulfilled for his disciples.

THE IMAGE OF MOTHER

Paul in his first letter to the Thessalonians in chapter 1: 7-12 uses the parental image of mother and father, to describe his ministry and that of Silvanus and Timothy as Thessalonica was a relatively young Church, and these pastoral images appropriately describe their ministry amongst them.

C. Cocksworth mentions Gregory the Great's "On The Pastoral Charge", in which he also uses the images of mother and father for the priest. "Gregory talks of the capacity of mothers to give birth and to nurture life."[12] An appropriate analogy to describe Paul and his associates as they were the spiritual mothers of the Thessalonian Christians. He also points out that Gregory the Great, "speaks of the priest as someone who has a mother's bosom and who can 'wash away by the comfort of exhortation and the tears of prayer', the troubles that overwhelm their charges."[13]

In 1 Thessalonians 1: 7 - 8 we read, "But we were gentle among you, like a nurse taking care of her children. So being affectionately desirous of you, we were ready to share with you not only the gospel of God but also our very own selves, because you had become very dear to us." Here one of the dominant features of the ministry of Paul and his associates was gentleness. Knowing how aggressive Paul was before his conversion we can only marvel at this Christ-like quality which he now displays. For all his stridency in defending Christian truth from false teachers he shows the ability to conduct affectionate and close relationships with these Christians, as indeed he also did with the Philippian Church. In writing to correct the Christians at Galatia Paul also refers to them maternally in Galatians 4: 19 as, "My little children with whom I am again in travail until Christ be formed in you." As we see how the young Thessalonian Christians were very dear to Paul and his associates, we can discern that this was a reflection of how precious they were to the Lord. In effect they were reflecting the pastoral heart of God and Christ towards them.

The close parental bond that had been established between these Christians and Paul and his associates, is reflected by their motherly devotion to them in 1 Thessalonians 1: 7-9. C. Cocksworth says, "...the energy of motherhood and the willingness of mothers to risk their lives in the giving of life are strong and powerful pictures of the calling of a priest."[14] Derek Tidball also quotes John Calvin on motherhood, "a mother in rearing her children reveals a wonderful and extraordinary love, because she spares no trouble or effort, avoids no care, is not wearied by their coming and going, and gladly gives her own life blood to be drained"."[15]   Paul and his associates gave themselves unreservedly to the Thessalonians much like a mother would to her children.

Tidball also compares the motherly devotion of Paul and his associates to that of a 'mother wet nursing' her own children.[16] This motherly image is also a reflection of God's feminine and motherly qualities.   We see this in Isaiah 49: 15-16: "Can a woman forget her suckling child that she should have no compassion on the son of her womb? Even these may forget but I will not forget you. Behold I have graven you on the palms of my hands."   We also glimpse this in Hosea 11: 1-2, "When Israel was a child I loved him and out of Egypt I called my son.....yet it was I who taught Ephraim to walk, I took them up in my arms".   In our generation the image of God as mother along with inclusive language about God is increasingly prevalent. Women priests are also now part of the landscape of the Church.   Moreover women usually outnumber men in church life. Here the challenge for the priest and for the people of God as a royal priesthood, is to allow the Holy Spirit to nurture the feminine qualities of God in their pastoral ministry, especially if they are a man; and to also nurture qualities of whole hearted devotion, gentleness and close relationships.

THE IMAGE OF FATHER

Anyone who has had the privilege of helping someone to respond to Christ in effect becomes a spiritual father to them. It is obviously easier to identify oneself as a spiritual father or mother depending on which sex we are. So in 1 Thessalonians 1: 11 it comes as no surprise to read about the relationship between the Christians at Thessalonica and Paul and his associates in the following way, "For you know how like a father with his children, we exhorted each one of you and encouraged you and charged you, to lead a life worthy of God, who calls you into his own kingdom and glory." While women have enjoyed considerable emancipation after centuries of male domination, we might well reflect that in our generation it is men who are now often undervalued and therefore a fresh focus on a fatherly spiritual role may well be timely.

In seeking a contemporary understanding of the role of father for both the priest and the people of God as a royal priesthood, the model of God as father is still very relevant. This may be particularly appropriate for those who did not have fathers who were a good role model. At the same time understanding Paul's perception of the fatherly role they adopted towards the Christians at Thessalonica, can help the priest and the people of God in their formation in this way. Tidball informs us that the Roman father was a powerful person with legal and financial authority over his children. Moreover fathers not only had rights, they had very significant responsibilities towards their children. These included guarding, providing, nurturing and teaching them.[17] Coming from a Greek patriarchal society myself, this description is not widely off the mark even in the 21st Century. In Paul's day and in Greek culture, parents would expect deference and respect from their children even when they were adults.

The first lesson the priest and the people of God can learn from Paul's use of the pastoral image of father, is that they nurtured a close relationship with the Thessalonian Christians. They made it their responsibility to initiate this close parental bond with each one in a personal way. Just as children demand their parents' time, love and attention, so too these young converts would have needed the same things in order to grow spiritually. Left to their own devices to look after themselves, they may well have faltered and not made much progress in their faith. The second lesson they can learn from Paul's use of the pastoral image of father is that of encouraging and exhorting these young Christians. This would have involved teaching, offering guidance and encouragement to them. In order that they might lead a Christ-like life which is pleasing to the Lord (1 Thess: 2: 12). The third lesson the priest and the people of God can learn from Paul's use of the pastoral image of father comes in chapter 2: 10: "You are our witnesses and God also, how holy and righteous and blameless was our behaviour to you as believers." Paul and his associates were setting these young Christians a role model as an example to follow. Just as parents nowadays expect their children to behave in a certain way so as not to embarrass them, so too Paul had no hesitation in setting an example for the Christians to follow. Elsewhere he says in 1 Corinthians 11:1, "Be imitators of me as I am of Christ Jesus."

Setting an example as a father figure for the priest and the people of God, helps to reflect to those they are caring for an example of God's fatherly love and concern. For central to the Christian faith is Jesus' teaching that we are able to relate to God in that personal intimate way, "Abba" - father. While the analogy of "mother" and "father" for the priest and the people of God may be appropriate in relating to Christian adults new to the faith, or relevant to their relationship with young people there is the danger this may become a sentimental image. Therefore they always looks to nurture peoples' faith by pointing them firmly to God and Christ, so that they might also nurture their relationship with them and learn to depend on them too.

5

BIBLICAL IMAGES OF PRIESTLY FORMATION

THE IMAGE OF PIONEER OF FAITH

It is indisputable that the starting point for appreciating the importance of faith in the Christian life is connected to our salvation through Christ. Ephesians 2: 8-9 encapsulates this belief: "For by grace you have been saved through faith and this is not your own doing, it is the gift of God. Not because of works, lest anyone should boast." Faith in God and what He has done through Christ is the foundation of our Christian lives.

It is one of the privileges as well as one of the priorities of the priest, to teach the people of God that through the gift of faith they can take hold of God's promises and blessings in scripture; and that living by faith is walking with God and learning to discover that He is trustworthy in their journey together. He/she also teaches God's people that in their pilgrimage the Lord will stretch and test their faith, sometimes to extreme limits, so that it can be refined as they discover new depths of trust in their walk with God. The priest also teaches them in the changing circumstances of life to keep their faith firmly focused on God and His character. To trust in His steadfast love and faithfulness even when they encounter difficulties or when they find it hard to reconcile them with their Christian faith. He/she also teaches the people of God by faith, to focus on who they are in God's sight, beloved children of God and friends of

Christ. The priest shares this responsibility with other lay leaders amongst the people of God as a royal priesthood. In 2 Timothy 2: 2-3 Paul instructs Timothy saying, "What you have heard from me before many witnesses, entrust to faithful men who will be able to teach others also."

Faith as understood in the New Testament involves a living relationship with God and Christ. A relationship which seeks to incorporate and put into action in our everyday lives the very truths that we believe as Christians. As young Evangelical Christians we were taught a definition of faith, "Forsaking all I take him." One which I think it is hard to improve on. This sums up the essence of the Christian faith which is to live for Christ and honour God. However the perennial danger and temptation for the priest and the people of God, is for their faith to become fossilized and remain merely a set of beliefs that does not have any impact or relevance in their lives. Therefore it is prudent for them to express their faith in practical ways in both the church and in the community. It may well be that a balanced approach is to have one commitment to their church during the week and one in their community too.

For the priest involved in serving the Lord there are innumerable opportunities to be involved in ministry and the same is true for the people of God. Here an insidious erosion of the essence of their faith can take place. This prevents faith from being an expression of a living, vibrant relationship with God and Christ, so that it is substituted by human activity. This deception is subtle and can prevent their faith from deepening and maturing. The antidote is to ensure that as a priority in the regular routine of church life, they are seeking to nurture a living relationship with God and Christ.

In the Autumn of 2002 on retreat at Folkestone having had a roller coaster experience due to the ongoing impact of post viral fatigue, the Lord reminded me of the importance to have implicit trust in him; even when I couldn't understand everything that had happened to me and when I was still living with major issues this had raised in my faith, for which I had no convenient or simple answers. The Lord reminded me of His call to have an unswerving faith in Him and not in myself, or in my efforts to work out answers concerning the way ahead for the future. His exhortation was not to put my trust in my own insight or ability or effort but to completely trust in Him. I returned from that retreat at peace about these issues and the future, knowing it was a question of facing each one a step at a time and trusting the Lord to be integrally involved. For the priest and the people of God their faith is forged and formed as they learn to walk in obedience and trust, and serve the Lord without necessarily seeing the future mapped out in its entirety; and at times living in what seems to be the ambiguity of their circumstances. Ultimately through this the Lord teaches His people not to trust in their own faith or themselves, but to ensure their trust is firmly in Him and in the truth that He is trustworthy.

For the priest and for those in lay leadership amongst the people of God, this involves maintaining a living vibrant relationship with God and Christ, so that their faith is nurtured by the Trinity from their reservoirs of spiritual life. In turn these leaders can encourage the people of God to also do the same so that their faith may deepen too. When the priest and lay leaders fail to nurture their relationship with God and Christ, their faith never really deepens or matures. Consequently they are unlikely to lead God's people into experiencing the spiritual blessings and benefits which is their inheritance of their faith in Christ.

The challenge for the priest and lay leaders amongst the people of God is to become pioneers in faith, so that their faith continues to grow and mature. Nurturing such faith demands spending time listening to what God is saying through the Scriptures and in prayer. This also means being obedient to carrying out God's vision and will for the church, for their own lives and for the community which may involve trusting God in new ventures. Scripture can provide many such examples of faith although the supreme example is Christ himself. In Hebrews 12: 2 Jesus is described as "The pioneer and perfecter of our faith." This aspect of Jesus' faith is a neglected jewel in the Christian tradition. However we can readily see that Christ was indeed an extraordinary pioneer of our faith, for in obedience to God's will he was willing to step out in faith, to be born as a baby and live a human life. The final and perfect expression of his supreme act of faith was to put his absolute trust in God by dying on the cross. These were extraordinary steps in his pilgrimage of faith as Christ had no previous human experience in his life as God, from which to launch his journey of faith into our world.

Christ left us an example of what is involved in being a pioneer of faith and for him this involved stepping into previously unknown territory in his incarnate life as the Son of God on earth. For Christ this meant having faith in God and trusting that He would be in control over his circumstances, as he was obedient to His will. For Abraham this involved leaving behind his own country and trusting God to fulfill His vision for his life. For David this meant trusting God to take him from shepherd boy to king. For the priest and the people of God today this means having an adventurous faith, which lives in openness to the plans God may have for them in their local church and for the community.

THE IMAGE OF BUILDER

The apostle Peter in his first letter in chapter 2: 5 exhorts God's people by saying, "And like living stones be yourselves built into a spiritual house."   A similar analogy is used by Paul in Ephesians 2: 19-20 when he says, "So then you are no longer strangers and sojourners, but you are fellow citizens with the saints and members of the household of God, built upon the foundations of the apostles and prophets, Christ Jesus himself being the cornerstone, in whom the whole structure is joined and grows into a holy temple in the Lord: in whom you are also built for a dwelling place of God in the Spirit." Here the clear implication is that God's people are in the process of being built into a "spiritual house" and into a "holy temple".

Obviously this is not a reference to the Church as God's physical building project, but it is analogous to a spiritual building project and this highlights the potential of the spiritual growth of the people of God. The analogy also implies the possibility that spiritual growth may not necessarily happen unless those involved in the building process build this spiritual house in the right ways. In 1 Corinthians 3:10-11 St. Paul likens himself to a master builder when he says, "According to the grace given to me, like a skilled master builder I laid a foundation and another man is building upon it. Let each man take care how he builds upon it. For no other foundation can anyone lay than that which is laid, which is Jesus Christ."

In this context we may liken the priest and the people of God as a royal priesthood, to skilled master builders who are building up the body of Christ as a "spiritual house and temple". In 1 Corinthians 3: 6-7 just before Paul refers to himself through this building anology, he makes a very important point to the Corinthian Christians about growth. He says "I planted, Apollos watered but God gave the growth. So neither he who plants nor he who waters is anything, but only God who gives the growth." Here he is rebuking the spiritually immature Christians who were attaching themselves to certain leaders because they thought they had a superior spirituality. Paul reminds us it is God who by his grace gives growth to His people that they may grow into a "spiritual house and temple."

One of my favourite television programmes is "Grand Designs". This hour long show involves two people usually a husband and wife building their dream home. Often these couples buy an old property, not necessarily a house and rebuild it to their specifications. To turn their vision into a reality they hire an architect who consults them about their design and then draws up plans for the builders to follow. Before an existing property can be rebuilt the architect assesses what is structurally sound, what needs to be repaired and what requires strengthening. Only then can the dream home proceed to be constructed. This preliminary assessment process in "Grand Designs" gives us some clues about building the people of God into a "spiritual house and temple". As the priest and the people of God seek to become skilled master builders they may well ask, "How can they arrive at their vision for building up God's people?" Building up God's people as a spiritual structure is a corporate issue which seeks to enable the Church to grow and mature. Initially this is not about seeking a vision about re-ordering or the future direction of the church, instead this building project addresses something much more fundamental.

The foundation of this building project can be discerned from the book of Acts, by seeing how the apostles went about building up the first Christian communities. In Acts chapter six, we learn one of the practical details of the church which involved the distribution of provisions began to distract the apostles, so they delegated this task to other members within the fellowship. We read in chapter 6: 2-4, "And the twelve summoned the body of the disciples and said, "It is not right that we should give up preaching the word of God to serve tables. Therefore brethren pick out from among you seven men of good repute, full of the Spirit and of wisdom, whom we may appoint to this duty. But we will devote ourselves to prayer and the to the ministry of the word." In Acts 6: 7 we see the result of this decision, "And the word of God increased: and the number of disciples multiplied greatly in Jerusalem and a great many of the priests were obedient to the faith". The apostles' devotion to prayer and the word of God was the central feature of their vision, for building up the people of God into a "spiritual house and temple". Building the people of God in this way begins with a profound corporate commitment to prayer and preaching and teaching the word of God, especially by the priest and those in positions of lay leadership amongst the people of God. A priority commitment to these things allows the Lord by his grace, to give growth to His people as a "spiritual house and temple."

As the priest and the people of God think about becoming master builders, surveying and correctly assessing the state of the "spiritual structure" of the fellowship, is absolutely vital and means investigating the history of the church. This involves consulting church members to see what previous pastors built, to examine the foundations they laid and the vision they pursued. This includes prayerfully discerning which parts of the "spiritual structure" of the fellowship are unsound and are in need of repair and also which parts are weak and require strengthening. In exploring the history of the fellowship they can learn whether any major issues of contention or conflict were left unresolved, or whether any major corporate or individual issues occurred which were never satisfactorily resolved and which may have left a negative spiritual legacy in the infrastructure of the church. At the same time they can seek to identify which parts of the structure are sound and can be consolidated. Wisdom to discern and accurately assess the condition of the "spiritual structure" of the fellowship is crucial to prayerfully developing a corporate vision under God, for building up God's people as a "spiritual house and temple."

The other outstanding building infrastructure we can perceive from the first Christians is the quality of their corporate life from Acts 2: 42-47. Obviously these first Christians did not have their own church buildings as they met in one anothers homes, and neither did they have the distraction of running a church building which often can resemble a small business. Freed from this distraction we see many practical expressions of the spontaneous "spiritual structure" which the Lord was building with these first Christians. In Acts 2 we perceive their unity: their practical generosity: their generous hospitality: their commitment to corporate worship: prayer: fellowship and teaching. We also readily perceive that they had glad and joyful hearts. All this spontaneous overflow resulted in a powerful social and evangelistic witnesses as the Lord added daily new Christians to the Church.

The work of the Holy Spirit was central and crucial in these corporate activities. In this embryonic church we do not perceive individualistic expressions of the Christian faith in the lives of these believers. It goes without saying that one of the biggest challenges facing the Church of England today, is for the priest and the people of God as a royal priesthood to become master builders and allow the Holy Spirit to build them up into a vibrant Christian community, that transcends a class or cultural expression of church life.

THE IMAGE OF NAVIGATOR

Over 40 years ago as a boy in Sunday school I used to sing a chorus about navigation, although like many choruses and hymns we sang I cannot remember that its meaning was ever explained to us. Only as I have come to write on the formation of the priest and the people of God as navigators, has this evocative image of Jesus as the pilot and the navigator of our lives surfaced from my memory. The chorus went something like this.

> Do you want a pilot signal then to Jesus
> Do you want a pilot bid him come on board.
> For he will safely guide across the ocean wide
> Until at last you reach the heavenly harbour.

It is reassuring for both the priest and the people of God as a royal priesthood, that Christ who is the head of God's Church, is also the one who can direct it to its ultimate destination, the heavenly city of God, the new Jerusalem. En route on this eschatological journey Christ helps them to chart their course and by his Spirit enables them to steer the Church in the right direction.   Along the way   he helps them to avoid the treacherous waters of life that might drown their faith and overwhelm them.

C. Cocksworth mentions that one of Gregory the Great's favourite images for the priest was that of navigator and he points out that the priest's pastoral calling is to be alongside people as they face "a storm of the soul", in which the vessel of the heart is ever tossed by gusts of feeling. Much of his advice is about helping people find their way through the difficult times of life and to steer their way through temptation and testing. He also mentions that "navigator" is a good image for the priest, as it recognizes that Christian experience is never stationary and that they steer us through the vicissitudes of life.[1] I suspect though that both the priest and the people of God have at times in their lives felt as if they have been becalmed, without being able to discern the direction of God's Spirit in their lives.

Derek Tidball mentions that the early Church took up the image of Jesus as the pilot and he alludes to Clement of Alexandria quoting one of his homilies part of which begins, "the Church is like a great ship carrying through a violent storm those from many places, who seek to live in the city of the good kingdom. Think of God as the shipmaster. Think of Christ as the pilot."[2] He also points out that Alexander Maclaren once referred to Jesus as the "Pilot of the Galilean lake", who will guide our frail boat through the wild surf that marks the breaking of the sea of life on the shore of eternity.[3] Tidball continues to point out that the image of the pastor as a pilot or navigator, is only mentioned once in scripture and unfortunately has been translated in a misleading way. This reference comes in 1 Corinthians 12: 28 and is one of the gifts of the Spirit and the Greek word is "kyberneseis". This is frequently translated as a gift of administration, but he points out that it was the word used by the Greeks to speak of the art of government, of guiding the ship of state. It is therefore the gift of helmsmanship, of steermanship or of navigation. The "kyberneseis" was the person with his hand on the tiller.[4]

The priest and the people of God in cultivating the Spirit's gift of navigation, have to learn to recognize the different ways that the Lord guides the Church and learn to discern God's voice as he directs them. This involves a life rooted in the rhythm of prayer and being in God's presence, becoming immersed in scripture so that they become sensitive to hearing God's voice and prompting in their hearts and minds. Tidball helpfully highlights some factors that are integral to providing direction in church life. He mentions that to pilot the Church requires, "A knowledge of the Lord and his Word. A knowledge of the Church and its ways. A knowledge of people and their make-up. A knowledge of the world and its state."[5] The challenge for the priest and the people of God is to be in partnership at the helm of the Church.

The gift of navigation is refined in the soil of experience and is also rooted in the Spirit's gift of deep discernment. As God's people seek to provide direction to church life and all its associated ministries, it is indispensable to discern God's leading and what he has to say on issues. The challenge to the priest and the people of God as navigators is to discern which ideas and initiatives are of the Lord, as ultimately they aim to navigate with the mind of Christ and discern the will of God. Integral to discerning the right destination to sail towards in the wind of the Spirit, they have to learn to recognize "the divine discontent" which can steer them in the Lord's direction. "Divine discontent" puts them in touch with the pulse of God's heart and reveals that He is not content to keep them standing still, or wandering around in circles or even going in the wrong direction in church matters. Just as dissatisfaction and discontent in other areas of our lives can act as a catalyst for transformation, so too "divine discontent" can reveal God's dissatisfaction and His direction for the church.

As navigators knowing the direction to take and which course to steer towards, may also involve understanding the history of their church and seeing what direction was previously taken and what vision was built upon, as these things can contribute to the process of discernment. David Lonsdale says something similar. "Discernment has to do with giving shape and direction to our lives in the present as we move into the future. But our lives already have a shape and a direction given to us, by the circumstances of the past and the choices we have made in those circumstances. The past, in the sense both of our personal past and of the corporate past we have shared with others, has made us what we are."[6]

While the priest and the people of God as navigators seek to guide all aspects of church life, it is important to cultivate an attitude of trust and an openness towards the Lord, as he seeks to guide them by the wind of His Spirit. They would be prudent to remember that wisdom in taking the right direction and choosing the right destination, may not always be the seemingly obvious choice to make. Proverbs 3: 5 exhorts us to, "Trust in the Lord with all your heart and do not rely on your own insight. In all your ways acknowledge him and he will make straight – direct your paths." As navigators who seek to steer God's Church, they are exhorted to submit their own insight and perception to the Lord and see whether He confirms this or changes it. This involves unreservedly placing themselves in God's hands, ensuring that their motivation is for God's glory not for building up their own egos and that they navigate a course according to God's principles and His ways. This involves being diligent so that the prevailing spirits of the age such as numerical success, spin doctoring, superficiality, idolatry, individualism, or being seen to be culturally relevant in their worship, do not infiltrate the life of the church and actually steer the priest and the people of God off course and hi-jack their destination.

THE IMAGE OF FREEDOM FIGHTER

We can trace the image of God as a "freedom fighter" way back to the Exodus in the Old Testament, where the Hebrews were oppressed by the Egyptians and God heard their plea and remembered his promise to Abraham and liberated them. God donned his mantle as a freedom fighter to set the Hebrews free as they were enslaved. Isaiah takes up the same theme of liberation in chapter 61: 1 and 3 when he prophetically utters of the Messiah:

The Spirit of the Lord God is upon me because the Lord has anointed me, to bring good tidings to the afflicted: he has sent me to bind up the broken hearted, to proclaim liberty to the captives and the opening of the prison to those who are bound. To grant to those who mourn in Zion - a garland instead of ashes, the oil of gladness instead of mourning, the mantle of praise instead of a faint spirit.

Jesus the Messiah, the Christ, was a liberator and freedom fighter following in the footsteps of Yahweh in the Old Testament. The people in Jesus' day lived in the hope and expectation that the promised Messiah would liberate them from the oppressive rule of the Romans. Freedom was an important make up in the psyche of the Jewish people firmly finding its foundation in the Exodus. They interpreted this freedom as territorial liberation from their oppressors. However the freedom Christ came to bring was primarily a spiritual freedom from the domain of the evil one and to give them the freedom to enter the Kingdom of God. This fundamental issue of freedom is inextricably connected to our salvation, as Christ the conquering warrior has triumphed over the principalities and powers by his victorious death on the cross. As a result Christ has set us free from the embrace of the evil one, (delivered us from the dominion of darkness and transferred us into the kingdom of his beloved Son – (Colossians 1: 13). And Christ has set us free from our sins and free from death and hell. In John 8: 31-32 Jesus said: "If you continue in my word you are my disciples and you will know the truth and truth shall set you free. So if the Son makes you free you shall be free indeed." Charles Wesley in his famous hymn, "And can it be that I should gain" in verse four, succinctly sums up this freedom from his personal experience:

> Long my imprisoned spirit lay,
> Fast bound in sin and nature's night:
> Thine eye diffused a quickening ray
> I woke the dungeon flamed with light.
> My chains fell of, my heart was free
> I rose went forth and followed thee.

A survey of Christ's ministry in the gospels readily reveals that he was indeed a freedom fighter setting people free from disease, from their sin, from long standing illness and from their addictive lifestyles. Mentioning some examples of the individuals who Jesus set free illustrates this liberating aspect of his ministry. In Mark chapter five we have three examples of this aspect of Christ's ministry. The first is of the man whose life was devastated and imprisoned by an unclean spirit (Mark 5: 1-13). The second is the healing of Jairus' daughter the ruler of the synagogue (Mark 5: 21-24 and 35-43).The third example is of the woman who had a flow of blood for twelve years, whom the physicians could not heal (Mark 5: 25-34). This is an extraordinary act of liberation as the woman merely touches the hem of Jesus' garment and is healed. Jesus publicly affirms her faith and publicly pronounces her healed of a disease which had excluded and isolated her from public life.

In Luke's gospel we read of the very moving account of the woman who washed Jesus feet with her tears, wiped them with her hair and anointed them. While she earned Simon the Pharisee's disapproval she received compassion and acceptance from Jesus and forgiveness and liberation from her sins (Luke 7: 45-48: 50): "You gave me no kiss, but from the time I came in she has no ceased to kiss my feet. You did not anoint my head with oil, but she has anointed my feet with ointment. Therefore I tell you her sins which are many are forgiven, for she loved much. And Jesus said to her, "Your sins are forgiven your faith has saved you go in peace."

There is the occasion when Jesus meets the Samaritan woman at the well in John chapter four. He breaks all conventional barriers by speaking to her and even asking her for a drink, but his concern goes beyond breaking the traditional customs of society. He discerns that this woman's lifestyle has not brought her fulfillment, so he engages her in conversation to give her the opportunity to be set free from her unfulfilling and addictive lifestyle. When Jesus reveals to her that he is the Messiah, something which is rare and unprecedented in the gospels, she is converted.

There are many other instances where Jesus sets people free in his earthly ministry. The last one to mention is one of the most striking and significant and this involves Jesus setting Peter from free his failure in denying him. Here Jesus takes the initiative to liberate Peter and sets him free to become the "rock". The apostle who was an outstanding leader in the early Church. It is still characteristic of Christ and his ministry today through both the priest and the people of God as a royal priesthood, to set people free and to liberate them. His ministry as described in Isaiah 61: 1-4 is still a contemporary one expressed through them. However just as Jesus delights to set people free today, we do well to remember that the devil still seeks to imprison people so that they lose their freedom. Therefore Jesus' ongoing ministry as a freedom fighter is the foundation for the priest and the people of God, to enable them to participate in this liberating ministry. The other crucial foundation is that God's people have to learn to become freedom fighters in prayer, so that through their corporate and individual prayers of authority in Jesus' name, empowered by the Holy Spirit, they can begin to liberate people from the devil's strongholds, and set them free from the things that enslave them.

THE IMAGE OF EVANGELIST

Having had a conversion experience and encountered Christ in a very real way thirty nine years ago when I was thirteen years old, as a teenager and young Christian I found that I naturally had an evangelistic heart. I imagine that anyone who has encountered Christ is given an evangelistic heart by the Holy Spirit, and this should come as no surprise to anyone as God has a missionary heart. Yet personally I have only led a small number of people to Christ. If to some extent this is representative of other Christians, it indicates there is something noticeably lacking in the way the Church facilitates the evangelistic outreach of the people of God as a royal priesthood. If this rings true for many Christians, it can be no surprise to the people of God if they do not fulfill their evangelistic instinct and potential.

One of my most memorable evangelistic experiences took place three years after becoming a Christian at a Covenanter camp in North Wales. As we were once again traveling there by train the thought occurred to me that during the camp I might be asked to share how I became a Christian At the same time the thought flooded through my mind that it wasn't as if I had been a particularly great Christian the past year, which might have been a reason for giving my testimony. Obviously my understanding of grace was much more limited in those days. As it turned out this was obviously a prompt from the Lord as I was subsequently asked to do this. Standing in front of around 150 boys and leaders seemed a rather daunting prospect. However I appreciated the time taken by the padre to discuss with me the questions he was going to ask me. As it turned out my testimony was apparently powerfully used by the Lord to speak to the other boys.

For the priest and the people of God as a royal priesthood, it is essential in their formation as evangelists to understand the underlying principals and theology about evangelism. A helpful place for doing this is from the book of Acts. In this we learn that God has an evangelist heart. Christ is an evangelistic Saviour and the Holy Spirit instigates evangelism. Evangelism is primarily a Trinitarian initiative and activity, which involves the co-operation and participation of the priest and the people of God.

In Chapter eight we see the Lord bringing together the Ethiopian Eunuch and Philip, who had the privilege of leading him to Christ. Here we see a simple model of Trinitarian evangelism. The Spirit was working in the Ethiopian's life giving him a spiritual hunger. Christ drew him to Isaiah 53 and God brought the seeker and the servant together. So that the seeker might come to Christ.

In Acts chapter ten we have the conversion of Cornelius. In effect this is the Gentile Pentecost. God speaks to both Cornelius and Peter preparing them to meet. Before Peter can be used in this evangelistic event, first he has to have a conversion experience himself! He has to be converted from his prejudice as a Jew against the Gentiles! Integral to this event is the obedience of Cornelius and Peter to what the Lord instructs them to do.

Before his conversion St. Paul had been resisting the conviction of the Holy Spirit to turn to Christ. Despite the fact God has been speaking to him through his encounters with the Christians he killed and persecuted, he was still blinded to the fact that Jesus was the Christ. I believe the Lord was prompting some Christians to pray for his conversion. As a result Christ revealed himself to Saul on the road to Damascus. Prayer and revelation are integral in the process of evangelism!

Roger Greenway gives an example of the evangelistic preparation of European pastors from a conference led by George Peters in 1980. At this conference he enquired how many of them had studied evangelism. Five had taken a course on the subject. Twenty had attended at least a one day workshop. However the vast majority had never had any formal instruction on how to do or organize evangelism. As a result Peters reflected whether there was any link between this lack of training and the major complaint throughout Europe, that the churches weren't growing. His own analysis was that the European churches and their pastors had never seen the connection between evangelism and pastoral ministry.[7] Although this example may seem somewhat outdated, this highlights what may be the glaring and obvious weakness, that is also linked to the decline in membership in the Church of England today.

We could ask to what extent are ministers being trained today by theological colleges in the area of evangelism, so that they automatically include this as part of their ministry in parish life? We could equally ask to what extent are they also trained to teach and facilitate the people of God in evangelistic outreach too?

Greenway having made observations over three decades in ministry is convinced that the separation in theory and practice, between "pastoral work and evangelism" is one of the chief sources of the Church's weakness and explains why churches do not grow. At the same time his study of the Scriptures have convinced him that the evangelistic dimension is so integral to the pastoral office, that to neglect this is rank disobedience to God. He concludes that the Bible makes evangelism not a pastoral option but a pastoral mandate.[8] He cites Jesus as being the perfect model of the godly pastor blending care for the faithful with the pursuit of the lost, and that as an itinerant preacher he sought out the scattered ones.[9]

This emphasis on the pastoral aspect of the life of the church involving evangelism comes across as refreshingly exciting, as for many Christians much of church life evolves around the life of their fellowship. The implication of considering Jesus' model is that pastoral work is not restricted to caring for Christians, but this automatically extends to embrace those outside the fellowship. The other natural implication of Jesus' model is that the both the priest and the people of God as a royal priesthood, are always looking out for lost souls and how to get in touch with them and bring them back home to God and Christ. To help this happen Greenway suggests the pastor and priest fulfills his leadership role in evangelism in three ways. He likens this to a three legged stool which will not stand unless all three legs are in place.

> * By teaching and preaching evangelism from the Scriptures.
> * By modeling evangelism in his lifestyle.
> * By organizing evangelistic thrusts into the community.[10]

Brad. J. Kallenberg researches the post modern world of society, to try to understand why the percentage of people responding to the gospel is nowadays so much lower than it used to be. He believes that in an age such as ours evangelism has become a cross-cultural task, and that we cannot take for granted any longer the common ground Christians once shared with Western culture. He suggests that belief in God or the deity of Christ, or the authority and inspiration of the Scriptures is no longer standard. As a result we must become students of the host culture as missionaries do. To discover how God's Spirit intends the gospel to become embodied in the new age. Missiologists call this "contextualisation".[11] As part of his research in seeing conversion from the human side he asks how it can be described in post modern terms. He thinks when simply viewed through a post critical lens conversion can be understood as involving:

> * The change of one's social identity.
> * The acquisition of a new conceptual (religious) language
> * The shifting of one's paradigm (world view).[12]

In effect Kallenberg is saying, the change in a person's identity is a social transformation that takes place when the gospel impacts their life, and a person begins to interpret the meaning of their life through the gospel community and its values. This involves interacting with gospel truths, a Christian community or stories from scripture that suggest a new paradigm (world view) for interpreting, understanding and finding meaning in their lives. He says:

> And by understanding one's place in the story of the gospel.... because this story line is lived out by the community of Christ-followers, the new convert's identity is necessarily social: one cannot identify oneself as a Christ-follower and avoid identifying oneself with the believing community that is seeking to embody the gospel in both its words and in its life together. The first lesson for evangelism to be gleaned from post critical philosophy then, is the importance of embodying the story of Jesus in our communal life. Such a community provides the context that demystifies the gospel by making it concrete.[13]

The following is an interpretation of Stallenberg's acquisition of a new conceptual (religious) language. Viewing evangelism and conversion as a communal activity, means embracing others in conversation spoken of in our conceptual (religious) language. For it follows that if people are not familiar with stories from the Bible which embrace religious ideas and concepts of God, Christ and humanity, then we can naturally deduce that conversion includes the learning or acquisition of the appropriate language. So for example to speak of God as our heavenly father may be meaningless to someone whose experience of their earthly father was negative, as they cannot identify with this concept of God. Only as there is the opportunity in dialogue to ask questions about God's fatherhood and to also question God's fatherhood, can there be a shift in conceptual language that eventually leads to conversion.

It may well be that ultimately the priest and the people of God have to allow their present paradigm of evangelism, to be converted by the Trinity. For they take the initiative to call them into partnership to seek out the lost. It is a also a timely reminder that their conversion was due to the initiative of the Trinity, probably through the connection with a Christian community where they were able to experience the gospel and in time also a paradigm shift.

THE IMAGE OF HOLINESS

Rosalind Brown says, "among the priestly people of God presbyters are appointed to hold this fundamental calling of the Church before the people of God, and to nurture this calling by shaping and forming Christian communities to be the holy people of God."[14] This calling demands that we ask the question, "what exactly does the formation of the priest and the people of God as a royal priesthood in holiness actually involve?"

Attempting to define holiness is a good springboard for exploring this important religious concept. The New Bible Dictionary reminds us, "there is probably no religion without a distinction between the holy and the profane."[15] It goes on to mention that in Scripture holiness usually means separation, with regard to people who have been separated or set apart for God and his service.[16] Being set apart involves consecration to the Lord and his service. Alternatively a holy place or a holy people who have been sanctified by the Lord, involves not only being set apart for God, but also displaying the distinctive quality of the character of being holy. The New Bible Dictionary says, "the ethical aspect in holiness is the aspect most commonly applied to God. It is basically a term for the moral excellence of God."[17] The priest and the people of God in nurturing their call to be holy are aiming for that moral excellence, and look to leave behind the ingrained habits of sin. This is an integral part in the process of their formation in holiness.

In contrasting God's holiness to our sinful human nature we not only conclude that morally God is perfect, but that there is also no possibility of sin or evil within His character. In Scripture God's holiness indicates His absolute perfection. He can do no wrong. Commit no sin or any evil, as these things have no possibility of existence within the perfection of His being. God's call to His people to be a 'holy people', is found early on in His covenant relationship with them. In Exodus 19: 6 the Lord said to the Hebrews whom he rescued from slavery in Egypt, "And you shall be to me a kingdom of priests and a holy nation". This same thought is echoed in Leviticus 19: 2 when the Lord commands his people, "You shall be holy for I the Lord your God am holy". In this chapter we also see how sin separates people from the holiness of God, for if the Hebrews came into God's presence they would die and be consumed because of their sin and God's holiness. For the priest and the people of God as a royal priesthood, holiness speaks of and points to a life that reflects this characteristic quality of God. This implies a call to living a holy lifestyle which is a distinguishing characteristic of being God's people. This is echoed by Rosalind Brown when she quotes Richard Baxter who defines holiness as, "a devotedness to God and living for him."[18]

Arriving at a working definition of holiness without it being overtly couched in biblical language is a challenge. As holiness is a prevailing characteristic of God's being and character and there is no possibility of sin in the perfection of His being, we can deduce that God's holiness is also supremely a relational quality that demonstrates itself in the way He conducts a relationship with His people. Therefore holiness as lived and demonstrated by the priest and the people of God, has relational ramifications and is seen in the moral and ethical sphere of the relationships God's people are involved in, both within the Church and in the world.

Demonstrating holiness in their relationships in the Church and society is extremely important, as this acts as a sacrament showing they are the people of God. In seeking to reflect God's characteristic holiness we can for example focus on his righteousness, his justice and his respect for the worth of individuals. The priest and the people of God can live holy lives by relating to others and treating others, in the way that God relates to them and in the way in which he treats them. Ephesians 4: 22 – 32 is an indication of how holiness in our lives can be evidenced in our relationships with others. Here Paul is reminding the Ephesian Christians in verses 22-24 about putting off their old nature which is corrupt through deceitful lusts and being renewed in the spirit of their minds, created after the likeness of God in true righteousness and holiness. From verse 25 he then proceeds to give concrete examples of how to express this righteousness and holiness in their relationships with one another. In verse 29 onwards he translates this holiness in terms of the tone of their conversation, "let no evil talk come out of your mouth but only speech which is helpful to others." Paul then links grieving the Holy Spirit with Christians manifesting bitterness, wrath, anger, clamor and slander in their relationships with one another. Holy living and holy relationships are the opposite of these things.

Rosalind Brown suggests that one way of exploring holiness is through the framework of the evangelical virtues of poverty, chastity and obedience.[19] She perceptively goes on to say:

> Chastity is about living holy and faithful lives so that others may similarly live. It is about becoming a whole and a holy person at peace with ourselves and trustworthy for God and others. Chastity frees us in our relationships with one another, since we do not use or abuse another person for our own benefit, or sacrifice others for any cause.[20]

Although she is not specifically talking about sexual holiness I believe her comments are appropriate in this contemporary arena of life. Inevitably in today's society when the priest and the people of God are bombarded with suggestive images immersed in sexual overtones, appealing to their unholy desires, holy living is inextricably linked to learning to express the wholesome gift of our sexuality through the God given affection, friendship and love we all have. One of the things I supremely miss from my hairdressing days and from my former college and Greek friends, is that within both sets of friendships there was the natural freedom to express our sexuality in holy and wholesome ways, through affection and attachment which was fulfilling.

It is the inheritance of the priest and the people of God to learn to express their affection, friendship and love - an expression of their "holy sexuality" in their relationships with one another and within their community.

THE IMAGE OF WORSHIPPER

Undoubtedly one of the privileges and joys for the priest and the people of God as a royal priesthood, is their participation in worship together. One of the challenges they face is to comprehend the dynamics and theology concerning worship.

C. Cocksworth reminds us that the charge at ordination to the priest in the Church of England, is to lead God's people in prayer and worship and that this priestly call is to oversee the culture and ethos of worship in the Christian communities we serve, to have our eyes set with John Chrysostom on, "one end: the glorification of God and the edification of the Church."[21] This may well constitute a definition of worship and certainly sums up admirable aims. J. Gledhill, the Bishop of Southampton, sums up the wonder of worship as he gives his definition. "Worship is the response of the creature to the creator; to worship is the desire to give true worth to what is beyond our powers of appreciation. To worship is to be aware of the heavens declaring the glory of God: to worship is to be aware of the transcendence of God: the infinite distance between the maker and the made; and at the same time his immanence: to be part of a creation that longs to respond more properly to God at work within it."[22] Marva Dawn says, William Temple brings together this movement from God as the subject, to God as the object in this beautiful and comprehensive definition of worship:

> The submission of all our nature to God. It is the quickening of the conscience by His holiness; the nourishment of the mind with His truth; the purifying of the imagination by His beauty; the opening of the heart to His love; the surrender of the will to His purpose – and all of this gathered up in adoration, the most selfless emotion of which our nature if capable. [23]

In response to the question "For whom is worship?" she quotes Gaddy, "worship is for God Only! The chief aim of worship is to please God". The point of worship is to recognize that "God alone matters."[24]

We are probably aware the origin in English of the word "worship" is "worthship", which expresses the value placed on someone or something. Graham Kendrick alludes to the word "proskyneo" as the most commonly used word to describe worship in the New Testament, which means "to come forward to kiss"(the hand) and it denotes both the external act of prostrating oneself in worship and the corresponding inward act of reverence and humility.'[25] David Peterson says, "worship means by derivation "to attribute worth" which suggests that to worship God is to ascribe him supreme worth." However he perceptively points out that worship interpreted and understood in this way, may not have any thing to do at all with the particularity of biblical revelation.[26] The ultimate weakness of the derivation 'worthship' is that it depends on people making a subjective assessment of God's worth. Such worship may then inadvertently become false and idolatrous, in as much as it begins with and hinges on our assessment of God. Peterson's understanding of what constitutes worship leads him to observe:

> While worship is often broadly defined as our response to God....there is an important theological context to be considered when worship is presented in such terms....at one level we must discover from God's own self-revelation in Scripture what pleases him. We cannot determine for ourselves what is honouring to him. In particular we need to take seriously the extraordinary biblical perspective that acceptable worship is something made possible for us by God.[27]

And I would add on God's terms and in the way he prescribes. This is the starting point of worship and not our particular preference for a particular style of worship, for worship is primarily something we offer to God not to please ourselves. D. Peterson concludes in the introduction of his book, "..that the worship of the living and true God is essentially an engagement with him on the terms that he proposes and in the way that he alone makes possible."[28]

C. Cocksworth says, "the new liturgical world calls us to attend to the dynamics of worship. It asks us to think carefully about the flow of worship. It invites us to ease ourselves into the skin of the liturgy, to see it through its eyes, because it is only when we inhabit a liturgy that we can use it properly."[29] I would go one step further and say that the pre-requisite for inhabiting the liturgy, is that in the first place the priest and the people of God learn to be inhabited by the Trinity themselves. As they learn to be and feel at home with the Trinity this can help them to appreciate and inhabit the liturgy, and to penetrate its Trinitarian spirituality on a deeper level.

Robert Barron says of the priest, "the mystagogue is one who has been entrusted with the sacred symbols and given the responsibility of making them speak. He is the artist whose task is to make a liturgy a great dance expressive of God's grace, a stunning saga at the heart of which is God's embrace of every respect of our fallen humanity…the mystagogue artist, in image, symbol and story, presents the truth that is God's love in Christ and draws the worshiping community to share in it."[30] We may well ask how can this happen and what does the priest have to do to achieve this; and to what extent does this depend on intellect, academic ability, gifting, or the spiritual sensibility of the people of God?   No one of these things on their own is necessarily the answer to our question. Barron perceives with great discernment the heart of the matter when he says, "the mystagogue….. is someone who at the core of his/her being has been set on fire by God and invites others to catch the flame."[31] Similarly he says, "the believer is grasped, shaken, overwhelmed by that powerful force, which in Jesus Christ is revealed as wild, passionate, unconditional love."[32]

The priest and the priest and the people of God together, can learn to explore the dynamics of worship and the liturgy and comprehend the biblical and theological truths which constitute authentic worship. C. Cocksworth echoes a similar thought when he says, "this appreciation of the liturgical dynamics of worship requires a deeper appreciation of the theological dynamics of worship and theological in the fullest sense of the Trinitarian dynamics of God's life of worship."[33]

   Martin Selman observes, "since the whole of life belongs to the sphere of worship, worship is much more a way of life than a series of liturgical acts. Worship demands comprehensive commitment which cannot be limited to any particular day of the week, or be concerned with some kind of activities and not with others.......The prophets were especially keen to emphasize that the people could not split their lives into religious compartments, insisting that people's behaviour in matters such as politics, ethics, business and family life were an integral part of their worship before God (Isa:1: 13-18)."[34] Selman goes as far as to suggest that a routine approach to sacrifice in connection with worship in our everyday lives, is the reason why many Christians seem to miss the significance of sacrifice in the new Testament and he also believes the New Testament in fact increases rather than reduces the importance of sacrificial worship.[35] This is echoed in Romans 12: 1-2 where we are exhorted, "Present your bodies as a living sacrifice, holy and acceptable to God which is your spiritual worship. Do not be conformed to this world but be transformed by the renewal of your minds, that you may prove the will of God, what is good, acceptable and perfect." These verses indicate that worship is a total lifestyle.

   While the priest and the people of God as a royal priesthood undoubtedly understand worship involves more than what takes place on Sundays, one way of educating them about these things can be implemented by having a "Worship Advisory Team", which consists of people who represent different styles or traditions in worship. Such a team can explore the dynamics, theology and different styles of worship to contribute to the worshipping life of the fellowship. A "Worship Advisory Team" can for example:

> Purchase books on worship as a resource for home groups to use as study guides, and to provide the content of preaching series and for individuals to read themselves.

> The team could classify the different types of modern hymns and songs and ensure they were correctly used in the right context in worship.

> Team members could take it in turn to visit other churches of different styles and traditions of worship to see what might be learnt from them.

> The team could organize half days or evening sessions on worship, by a well known speaker on worship or expert in liturgy.

> The team could ensure that those involved in leading the worship of the church, take it in turn to go on conferences on worship each year.

> The team could invite feedback from the congregation about the worship, affirming what they value and making constructive suggestions about what might be improved.

The team could invite the congregation to ask any difficult or searching questions related to the issue of worship, which the "Worship Advisory Team" along with the clergy or ministry team can explore.

It is all too easy for the priest and the people of God to think they are immersed in the middle of the ocean of worship, and that they have achieved an excellence in their particular style and tradition. Yet in reality they may only really be paddling at the water's edge. Having an "Advisory Worship Team" can help to safeguard against such a false evaluation and wrong perception. The worship team can also explore the issue of false worship and be alert to how the prevailing spirits of our age may have infiltrated their worship. It can also act as a catalyst for experimentation in worship and provide an accurate feedback of the church's formation and pilgrimage in worship.

Marva Dawn in her substantial book, "A Royal Waste Of Time – The Splendour Of Worshipping God And Being Church For The World", addresses the needs of our being in worship by asking seven crucial questions, that both Christians and non Christians are likely to ask and seek answers to. She is convinced that worship immersed in God's splendour will meet these deep needs, especially if that worship includes the whole Church as a true community and the whole of the Scriptures as they form us with all their depth. These are her seven categories of meaning which the priest and the people of God would do well to take note of, if they want their worship to have depth and substance.

* Identity: who am I?
* Master story: how does it all fit together?
* Loyalty: to whom do I belong? Whom shall I trust?
* Values: by what shall I live?
* Power: how can I protect myself? How can I make my
  way over against others?
* Meaning: what is the purpose of my life?
* Hope: why should I go on?[36]

THE IMAGE OF OFFERING SACRIFICES

In the Levitical sacrificial system in the Old Testament as was
seen in chapter one, the priest's primary role was in offering
sacrifices to God. However in this chapter we also learnt that
Christ's offering of himself on the cross put an end to this
sacrificial system. This has been superceded by the type of
sacrifices the people of God as a royal priesthood are now able
to offer. We see from 1 Peter 2: 5 these sacrifices are now
primarily spiritual ones and are also related to all areas of our
lives: "and like living stones be yourselves built into a spiritual
house, to be a holy priesthood, to offer spiritual sacrifices
acceptable to God through Jesus Christ."

The issue and concept of sacrifice is an integral feature of
Jesus' life and ministry, and self sacrifice is a foundational
concept in his teaching on discipleship. We see this in Mark 8:
34 - 35 where Jesus says, "If any man would come after me let
him deny himself and take up his cross and follow me. For
whoever would save his life will lose it; and whoever loses his

life for my sake and the gospel's will save it". Ian Bradley says, "Jesus' repeated emphasis on the importance of self-sacrifice as the foundation of discipleship is one of the most distinctive elements of his teaching........this call for the utter surrender of self is reinforced by his grim reminders to his disciples, that the reward to those who follow him will be suffering and servitude (Mark 10: 30, 44)."[37]

The precedent for a call to such sacrifice is based on the example of Christ himself. Philippians 2: 1-11 shows Christ sacrificing his status and glory as God, to become God's servant. Jesus also lays down his life for us as the good shepherd. The good shepherd who sacrificed his life for us in abandonment and obedience to the will of God. On the cross Christ as a sacrificial offering revealed to us the heart of the Father. For through the cross we see the sacrificing nature of God himself, in giving us His son. This is a supreme example to the priest and the people of God as a royal priesthood, as they learn to offer spiritual sacrifices acceptable to God through Jesus Christ. It is a timely reminder that spiritual sacrifices pleasing to God flow from the inner disposition of the heart, not just from outward rituals. At times offering such sacrifices to God may well be costly.

Martin Selman says, "sacrifice is not merely associated with worship, it lies at its very heart. This understanding has recently been expounded by S. W. Sykes who argues that the ideas, language and practices of sacrifice are central to the relationships that people enjoy with God. Since Christians express their relationships with Jesus most fully through worship, which in biblical thought is symbolized externally and internally by sacrifice, sacrificial worship is the proper means for communicating the meaning of that relationship. Or to put it another way, the most profound way to show one's love for God in worship is to lay everything on His altar."[38]   This is a reflection of Jesus' relationship with his Father, which was consistently expressed as the sacrificial worship, of a loving and obedient son. M. Selman adds, "the implications of this for the Christians are far - reaching. Once one becomes aware of the possibility that sacrifice is about the expression of a loving relationship, neither worship nor sacrifice can be confined any longer to mere action, whether performed in church or elsewhere. On the contrary worship in a biblical way, makes a claim on every part of a Christian's life. Worship that is acceptable to God will be influenced by sacrificial principles at the most fundamental level."[39]

In the formation of offering spiritual sacrifices to God, what sort of sacrifices might the priest and the people of God offer up to the Lord in their everyday lives? Romans 12: 1-2 indicates that the presentation of their bodies to God by not being conformed to the world's way of living, is a living sacrifice, holy and acceptable to God and constitutes their spiritual worship. An obedient life lived in the way of holiness in the world in which they work and live, is an integral aspect of a spiritual sacrifice which the people of God are able to offer to the Lord. This involves consecrating their lives in serving Him and doing His will, which also constitutes a spiritual sacrifice offered to God. Steve Walton says, "instead of part of life being the sphere of the sacred, the whole of life becomes sacred for the believer.....The sphere of worship for the Christian is not primarily the congregation, but the world in which Christ is to be served."[40]

In 1 Peter 2: 9 we see that witnessing for the priest and the people of God may also be seen in terms of offering a spiritual sacrifice to God, "….you are a royal priesthood…that you may declare the wonderful deeds of him who called you out of darkness into his marvelous light." Paul in Romans 15: 16 also alludes to offering a spiritual sacrifice in terms of witnessing to the gospel, "…because of the grace given me by God to be a minister of Christ Jesus to the Gentiles in the priestly service of God, so that the offering of the Gentiles might be sanctified by the Holy Spirit." In this verse Steve Walton observes that there is a clustering of sacrificial language "priestly service" – hierougounta, "offering" – prosphora, "acceptable" – euprosdektos and "sanctified" – hegiasamene.[41]

Prayer offered up by the priest and the people of God may also be seen as a priestly ministry and a spiritual sacrifice. This can be seen in Revelation 5: 8 which speaks of the prayers of the saints as golden bowls full of incense and also in Revelation 8: 3: "And another angel came and stood at the altar with a golden censer, and he was given much incense to mingle with the prayers of all the saints upon the golden altar before the throne." Incense rising to the throne of God is an allusion to sacrificial language from the Old Testament in Exodus 30: 1. In thinking of prayer as a spiritual sacrifice we saw in chapter one, through Christ we can draw near to the throne of grace and have access into the presence of God. Prayer may therefore be interpreted as offering a spiritual sacrifice to God, as drawing near is symbolic of priestly language in the Old Testament.

Steve Walton says, "giving is also described in terms of sacrificial language, where Paul in Philippians 2: 17 sees himself as, "being poured out as a libation upon the sacrificial offering of your faith." He also sees the gift of money by Epaphroditus to Paul in Philippians 4: 18 from the same perspective of sacrificial terminology. "I am filled having received from Epaphroditus the gifts you sent, a fragrant offering, a sacrifice acceptable and pleasing to God."[42] From the inference of Paul pouring out his life as a libation upon the sacrificial offering of the Philippian's faith, we may also perceive that for the priest and the people of God, laying down their lives is also seen as a sacrificial offering to the Lord. Laying down their lives need not be interpreted in terms of dying, but as a spiritual offering as they give their lives by serving God and others.

Praise is another spiritual sacrifice for the priest and the people of God, to offer up to the Lord. Some of the Old Testament sacrifices were principally thanks and praise, for example the peace offering in Lev: 7: 11-18. The writer in Psalm 50:14 says, "Offer to God a sacrifice of thanksgiving" and this is also echoed in Psalm 116: 17. Hebrews 13: 15 also exhorts us, "Through Christ then let us continually offer up a sacrifice of praise to God, the fruit of lips that acknowledge his name."

THE IMAGE OF SUFFERING

At some time or another suffering is likely to be an integral feature of everyone's life and there may be a number of reasons why this happens. Suffering can be a result of the natural or tragic events of life such as bereavement or a terminal illness, or a tragedy. It may also result from other people's actions or sin or indeed be a result of our own actions, mistakes or sin.

For the priest and the people of God as a royal priesthood, suffering at times may be seen to be connected to their faith and at times may be attributed to the activity of the evil one. On occasions suffering may even be seen to come from the hand of the Lord, as he works through the events in their lives. However great discernment has to be exercised before they attribute specific suffering in their lives, to the hand of the Lord.

Whatever the cause of their suffering it may be argued that the determining factor is their response to this, which in turn influences the way they are shaped by what they go through. Hopefully many Christians in and through their suffering will find support from their family, their friends and from the people of God in their fellowship. A reflection of God's goodness. For the priest and the people of God it may well be helpful to understand how the Lord can use their formation through suffering, to bring about good in their lives and to further his purpose in the lives of His people. Romans 5: 3 – 5 indicates what the Lord can do in their lives through suffering. "More than that we rejoice in our sufferings, knowing that suffering produces character and character produces hope and hope does not disappoint us because God's love has been poured into our hearts by the Holy Spirit, which has been given to us." The implication of the truth contained in these verses is that for Christians God can use their suffering to build up their faith and produce the qualities of endurance, character and hope in their lives. At times God's people may be puzzled why the Lord allows them to suffer and this may cause some people's faith to fail. However difficulties and suffering can also result in their faith being strengthened as they learn to trust the Lord through this formative process.

In the first chapter of 2 Corinthians we can readily discern some major reasons why the Lord sometimes allows suffering to occur in the lives of his people. In verse eight Paul speaks of difficulties and the ensuing suffering as an affliction so utterly painful, that he and his colleagues were unbearably crushed and despaired of coming out of it alive. The underlying issue of importance from Paul's testimony, is that on reflection he interpreted this affliction and suffering as coming directly from the hand of the Lord. Equally his perception of the reason for this life threatening affliction, shows the formation that the Lord accomplished in their lives through the suffering he allowed. In verse nine as Paul reflects on this particular aspect of suffering, the Holy Spirit shows him that the Lord was teaching them to rely on him. In verse three and four he is also shown by the Spirit that through this traumatic experience and ensuing suffering God was manifesting his comfort in their lives, so that in turn they might comfort and support others in their suffering too. Moreover in verse five Paul also perceives that suffering as a Christian is also in some measure a sharing in Christ's suffering.

One of the lessons which I have painfully learnt in my formation through suffering both as as a Christian and also a priest, is that the Lord may allow a weakness to develop in the lives of His people which causes them considerable suffering. At times this may be a silent and unseen inner suffering. For St. Paul this weakness was his thorn in the flesh and it was periodically so painful he saw it as a disadvantage and went so far as to ask the Lord to remove it. In 2 Corinthians 12: 7 – 10 we learn that the purpose in allowing Paul to have this weakness was that he might learn to rely on the Lord, and not become elated or conceited by the abundance of revelations the Lord had given him. His weakness however took him into a deeper dimension in his relationship with Christ than otherwise might have happened, and through this he experienced more of Christ's sustaining power. At times what we might consider constitutes a weakness in other people's lives, may in fact be holy ground and very precious to the Lord. A weakness which he has allowed to cause them considerable suffering. Suffering which will eventually bear the fruit of a Christ like character. Suffering through which the Lord will produce depth in their faith and through which the Lord may prepare and equip a person to serve him.

There may also be occasions in the lives of the priest and the people of God that are particularly traumatic and which they struggle to make sense of, and struggle to see the Lord's hand in what has happened. Although this suffering may not come from the hand of the Lord, what He accomplishes in their lives through this will probably be only be seen in retrospect. This painful formative process can lead to the refining of their suffering, through which the Lord will be able to comfort and touch other people's lives on a profound level.

In Hebrews 2: 10 we read, "For it was fitting that he, for whom and by whom all things exist, in bringing many sons to glory should make the pioneer of their salvation, perfect through suffering." Raymond Brown sees these words as initially bewildering because we know that Christ was morally perfect and sinless. He observes that the word translated perfect in verse ten, frequently appears in the letter to the Hebrews. He says, "it signifies the completion of a process" and "Christ's life and work were brought by suffering to a form of perfection and completeness which cannot have been possible without them."[43] He also observes that Christ became perfect in and through his obedience.[44]

Christ's obedience was evident throughout his life and ministry. But the full potential of this obedience was brought to absolute perfection, by his submission to the Father's will to die on the cross. There is a sense in which everyone's potential in life can only be realized through their being tested and stretched to the limit. The same is true concerning our formation in suffering. The priest and the people of God may potentially serve God to the ultimate limit of their faith, however this potential is only realized as their faith is stretched and tested and refined through various difficulties and suffering. Coming through these trials of faith contributes to the completion of the potential of their formation through suffering, and on occasions it is only through suffering that they are transformed and equipped to serve others. Through their suffering they can become bearers of God's redemptive purposes, as they offer this to the Lord and He then takes it, blesses it and ministers to others through it. Nicholas and Christine Henshall remind us:

> The Lord we follow, the Lord whose life we claim to share, is one whose only way to heal us was to be wounded and whose only way to real life was suffering and death. That is why – perhaps most importantly and most intangibly – the way of priesthood is a way marked with the wounds of Christ.[45]

THE IMAGE OF SERVANT

Servanthood is a central feature in the life of Christ and subsequently an integral aspect of the gospel, and also in the formation of the priest as well as the people of God as a royal priesthood. A traditional view might assume that the priest is primarily the one who serves amongst the people of God. But such an outlook fails to comprehend the call and challenge to the whole people of God in their formation as servants of Christ, one another and the world.

The example of Christ as God's servant and ours, embraces the heart of the gospel and epitomises the life and character of Christ. In Mark 10: 35 – 45, we have the context in which the disciples want to share in the glory of Christ and his kingly rule in the way they expect it to materialize. The image of rule which they focus on is one of power where they will be served by others. Jesus cuts through this gross misapprehension to teach them about greatness in the kingdom of God when he says in verses 42 – 45: "You know that those who are supposed to rule over the Gentiles lord it over them. But it shall not be so amongst you; but whoever would be great among you must be your servant and whoever would be first among you must be slave of all. For the Son of man also came not to be served but to serve, and to give his life as a ransom for many." Here Jesus turns the expectation, perception and values of the disciples upside down, as he teaches them that greatness is not achieved through domination or through having others serving them, but through their formation as servants and slaves to others.

The image of Jesus as God's servant and our servant, also influences the formation of all of God's people as servants. From Philippians 2: 1 – 8 we can perceive some of the truths which embody Christ's servanthood. From this passage we can see three attitudes which are central to Jesus' motivation and outlook as a servant. Firstly in verses 6 – 7 we can see his attitude towards God, in that Christ did not count equality with God a thing to be grasped, but emptied himself and gave up his equality, status and glory which he shared with God. This represents the mind and attitude of Christ. Here there is an unspoken reference to Adam who grasped at equality with God by eating of the fruit of the tree of knowledge of good and evil, where the temptation was to reach out to be like God (Genesis 3: 5). Secondly in verses 6 – 7 we see Jesus' attitude towards himself. Having laid aside his equality with God he took on himself the role of being God's obedient servant. Thirdly in verse 8 we see Jesus' attitude to us. He became our servant and secured our salvation by dying on the cross for us. These truths represent the heart and mind of Christ as a servant. Therefore the priest and the people of God in their formation as servants, are exhorted in these verses to embrace these attitudes of Christ. In chapter two verse three this attitude is to be one of counting others better than ourselves, rather than having selfish or conceited attitudes towards others. In verse four this attitude is seen by taking an interest in other people's lives, rather than just our own and in verse five the people of God are exhorted to have the mind of Christ which was that of a servant.

Another pivotal passage in grasping the essence of Jesus' servanthood, is found in the example when he washed the disciples feet in the last supper in John chapter thirteen. We know the servant of the household would traditionally have been expected to wash the visitor's feet, however as there is an element of secrecy in the supper they are sharing with Jesus, there is no one there to carry out this menial task. Yet Jesus their Lord and master willingly takes a towel and washes the feet of the embarrassed disciples, who probably struggled to comprehend the enormity of what he was doing. In hindsight we know that Jesus was teaching them by example that leadership is not about lording it over others. Instead leadership involves meekly serving others in humble down to earth ways, as we perceive their need. Isaiah 53 is another pivotal passage in comprehending the heart of Jesus as a servant. We know that Jesus' experience as a servant involved enormous suffering, which this chapter so movingly portrays. In this chapter we see his servanthood was not characterized or epitomized by comfort or self indulgence, instead Jesus plumbed the depths of heart breaking agony, rejection and scorn. Having become God's servant Jesus placed himself in the hands of others, surrendered control to them and was at their mercy. Yet as God's servant his trust firmly remained in the fact he was ultimately secure in the Father's hands.

The priest and the people of God through their formation as servants may find that as they surrender their lives to the Lordship of Christ, that at certain times they experience a greater degree of suffering as they serve the Lord. Equally the Holy Spirit through this process of formation will at times transform their motivation as servants, so that they also have the attitude of John the Baptist formed in them. He is reported in the gospel of John as setting this example before us in chapter 3:30. "He must increase, but I must decrease". As a servant John firmly pointed people to Christ and not to himself. This is the challenge to the priest and the people of God as they serve him.

This process of being formed as servants is beautifully and movingly portrayed for the priest and the people of God, in the "Parable of Bamboo" shared by Daniel O'Leary. "Once upon a time in the Western Kingdom lay a beautiful garden, and there in the cool of the day the Master of the Garden liked to walk. Of all the creatures in the garden, the most beautiful and most beloved was a gracious and noble bamboo tree. Year after year Bamboo grew yet more noble and gracious, conscious of the Master's love and watchful delight but always modest and gentle.

And often when the wind came to revel in the garden, Bamboo would cast aside her gravely stateliness to dance and play, merrily tossing and swaying and leaping and bowing in joyous abandon, leading the Great Dance of the Garden which delighted the Master. Now one day the Master sat down to contemplate his Bamboo with eyes of curious expectancy. Bamboo in a passion of adoration bowed her great head to the ground in loving greeting. The Master spoke; "Bamboo I would use you". Bamboo flung her head to the sky in utter delight. The day of days had come, the day for which she had been made, the day for which she had been growing, hour by hour, the day in which she would find her completion and her destiny. Her voice came softly: "Master I am ready. Use me as you will". "Bamboo" – the Master's voice was grave, "I would like to take you and – cut you down."

"Cut...me...down! Me...whom you, Master had made the most beautiful in all your garden. Cut me down! Not that, not

that. Use me for your joy O Master, but do not cut me down!"
"Beloved Bamboo" – the Master's voice grew graver still – "If I
do not cut you down I cannot use you". The garden grew
still....wind held his breath. Bamboo slowly bent her proud and
glorious head. Then came a whisper: "Master if you cannot use
me unless you cut me down...then...do your will and cut".
"Bamboo, beloved Bamboo, I need to cut your leaves and branch
from you also". "Master, Master, please spare me. Cut me down
and lay my beauty in the dust, but would you also take from me
my leaves and my branches?" "Bamboo, if I do not cut them
away I cannot use you". The sun hid his face. A listening
butterfly glided fearfully away. And Bamboo shivered in
terrible expectancy, whispering low, "Master, cut away".

"Bamboo, Bamboo, I would split you in two and cut out your
heart, for if I don't I cannot use you". Then was Bamboo bowed
to the ground. "Master, Master...then cut me and split me". So
did the Master of the Garden take Bamboo and cut her down and
hacked off her branches, and stripped off her leaves and cleaved
her in two and cut out her heart. And lifting her gently he carried
her to where there was a spring of fresh, sparkling water in the
midst of his dry fields. Then putting one end of broken Bamboo
into the spring and the other end into the water channel in his
field, the Master laid down gently his beloved Bamboo. The
clear, sparkling waters raced joyously down the channel of
Bamboo's torn body into the waiting fields. Then the rice was
planted and the days went by, and the shoots grew and the
harvest came. In that day was Bamboo once so glorious in her
stately beauty, yet more glorious in her brokenness and humility.
For in her beauty she was life abundant, but in her brokenness
she became a channel of abundant life to her Master's world".[46]

We can readily perceive through this moving parable, a picture of Jesus the servant in complete abandonment and submission to the Father's will. We also see Jesus' absolute faith in placing himself in the Father's hands as he goes to the cross. Faith which delighted and trusted in God to use him as a channel of blessing for others, even though ultimately it would cost him his life and bring excruciating pain, physically, emotionally and in his relationship with his Father. In this parable we also perceive a challenge to follow the example of Christ as servants in the Lord's hand. It is also a reminder to the priest and the people of God as a royal priesthood that as servants there is a eucharistic element to their formation which is etched in the words of consecration in the Communion service:

He took: He blessed: He broke: He gave.

Through this prayer we see that God took the life of Jesus which he offered to Him. God blessed his life. He then broke it on the cross and through Christ's risen life He gave life to others. The same eucharistic pattern is repeated in our lives. When the priest and the people of God offer themselves as servants to the Lord, through their abandonment and brokenness they too can be channels for the fragrance of Christ to flow to others.

THE IMAGE OF PROPHET

A good starting point for the priest and the people of God as a royal priesthood in thinking about their formation as prophets, is to briefly look at one or two examples from Scripture. In Deuteronomy 34: 10 we read, "And there has not arisen a prophet since in Israel like Moses, whom the Lord knew face to face". Wayne Crudem says:

> The main function of Old Testament prophets was to be messengers from God, sent to speak to men and women with words from God.[47]

The implication associated with this was that a prophet's words authentically carried authority, as his words were directly from God. Here we can readily make the connection with Moses being in the prophetic tradition, as he spent time with God and the Lord spoke to him and addressed His people through him.

Clifford Hill defines prophecy by saying:

> Prophecy was thus regarded as the revealed word of God. It was not the product of intellectual attainment or rational debate. Neither was it deduced through the processes of logical deduction. Prophecy was revealed truth that came directly from God. It was the word of God delivered by God to man. Thus prophecy was 'received' rather than produced by the human mind.[48]

The Old Testament prophets were God's messengers who spoke God's word to His people Israel, in the context of their covenant relationship with the Lord. As a prophet spoke God's word to His people this was a contemporary message, even if it contained a warning of judgment or spoke about consolation or hope. A prophet was not primarily predicting what would happen in the future, he was addressing the current spiritual and political life of God's people, in the context of their covenant relationship with the Lord.

However God's word to His people through the prophets, was not a fait accompli about what would happen in the present or the future. The outcome of the present and the future of God's people, was primarily dependent upon their response to His word through the prophets. We see an example of this in the life of Jeremiah, through whom the word of God to His people was a contemporary warning to repent of their idolatry and apostasy (forsaking the Lord for other gods – idols of wood and stone). Jeremiah spoke God's word to His people calling them to repent and return to the Lord, and renew their covenant commitment and relationship with Him. This message also contained a warning of judgment if God's people did not respond. Therefore Jeremiah also warned God's people that if they refused to repent and return to the Lord and rejected His word to them, then future judgment was on its way and they would be invaded by an enemy, a foe from the North. However one serious problem which confronted Jeremiah was the existence of false prophets, who were saying that everything was fine and in effect contradicting his message. There is a reference to them in Jeremiah 6: 14 where the Lord says: "they have healed the wound of my people lightly saying, "peace, peace" where there is no peace".

Integral to a prophet's gifting is seeing the political and spiritual condition of the nation from God's perspective. While the political and spiritual leaders in Jeremiah's day thought they were secure and in a period of prosperity, he saw that in God's eyes politically and spiritually they were in decline because of their idolatry and apostasy. A prophet is therefore one who stands in God's presence, is immersed in God's word and sees from God's perspective the reality of things as they are in the life of the nation and the Church. While Jeremiah challenged and confronted the political and spiritual leaders of his day, ultimately they had deluded themselves into having a false confidence in their religious heritage. They thought that because they were God's people they were exempt from the imminent judgment Jeremiah was warning them about.

Karl Rahner believes that in the Catholic Church, priesthood combines in one office the distinctive roles of the priest and prophet; with the priest presiding over the community's ritual worship and the prophet addressing the community in God's name and speaking God's Word.[49] Thomas Rausch says, "a prophetic priesthood is a priesthood given to the ministry of the word in its fullest sense. It is primarily kergymatic rather than liturgical, though it does not exclude the liturgical."[50] He quotes Michael Buckley who describes the prophetic dimension of priesthood in this way:

> A prophetic priesthood, one which was concerned to speak out the word of God in any way that could be heard, assimilated and incarnated within the social life of human beings, a priesthood which spoke with the religious experience of human beings and – as did the prophets of the Old Testament – coupled this care for authentic belief with a concern for those in social misery:[51]

The dual dimension of the priestly and the prophetic within priesthood in the Catholic Church, strikes a chord with the prophet's role in the Old Testament which also advocated justice for the poor and underprivileged.

As is so movingly seen in Jeremiah's life, a prophetic ministry also involves speaking with courage and challenging the established views of those in power. This involves speaking God's Word to His people and usually means confronting the idolatry and godless characteristics of the nation. For Jeremiah this involved challenging the political and religious leaders who were the people in power.

Walter Brueggemann argues that the old confrontational model of "prophet versus established power," is increasingly difficult to pull off as the Church in effect lacks the authority to do this. For that reason he believes this prophetic model of confrontation is not to be replicated, but the prophetic voice must embrace immense imagination to address contemporary circumstances.[52] He refers to O'Connor who discovered the imagination might accomplish much more; it might become the channel of visionary awareness.[53] He mentions that out of the crucial work of Paul Ricoeur on imagination, it became generally evident that texts – in particular biblical texts – are acts of imagination that offer purpose and hope: "alternative worlds: that exist because of and in the act of utterance".[54] For the prophetic consciousness sees things can and should be different and that is the essence of God's imagination and this involves the possibility of transformation. He believes that to participate in the Eucharist is to live in God's imagination.[55]

Brueggemann says:

> The task of the prophetic ministry is to nurture, nourish and evoke a consciousness and perception, alternative to the consciousness and perception of the dominant culture around us.[56]

He mentions for example that the liberation of the Hebrews in Egypt was nothing less than an assault on the consciousness of the empire, aimed at nothing less than the dismantling of the empire in both its social practices and its mythical pretensions. "Yahweh makes possible and requires an alternative theology and an alternative sociology."[57] That alternative theology and sociology is none other than the Kingdom of God – and where this is authentically lived out by the priest and the people of God, this is a truly prophetic voice and witness.

Kenneth Leech mentions the prophetic role of priesthood when referring to the call to be a watchman. He believes discerning the signs of the times calls for a vision of the world which sees through its illusion and its falsehood. He mentions that the image of the priest as revolutionary leader is not so absurd, and may help us to understand the nature of the priestly vocation of illuminating consciousness. For the priest is an agent for the illumination of the consciousness of the community he serves.[58]

Stephen Glover perceives the prophetic consciousness of the Church in an article he wrote in the Daily Mail. This is a summary of what he said. As the son of a vicar he remembers the Church as a forgiving one, yet one which also spoke with a clear and unambiguous voice on adultery, homosexuality and abortion. But there has been a loss of the old certainties on moral issues, which reflects the enormous shift that has taken place in social mores. As a result the Church no longer speaks with a clear and unambiguous voice. Far from defining and defending Christian values, the Church seems increasingly to kowtow to the values of the secular world. It now barely connects with the wider nation and has more and more taken the character of a sect, preoccupied with its own arguments and divisions. The Church nearly tore itself apart over the ordination of women and now it is on the verge of splitting on the issue of homosexuality. Our country was made and shaped by Christianity and the Church, yet that Church has withdrawn from our national life. It has lost its authority and respect. Let us hope, even pray, that it will one day stop talking to itself and speak to us.[59]

Regardless of whether we agree with Steven Glover, what should be taken seriously is that his perception may be an accurate reflection of how society in general views the Church of England. His words may prove to be prophetic, inasmuch as the Church has lost its prophetic consciousness and voice in addressing the nation. If the Church is indeed merely talking to itself, then it is a timely reminder that the priest and the people of God should be listening to God and hearing what He has to say to the Church and the nation. Only then will the Church rediscover its prophetic consciousness and courage, to speak in the name of the Lord.

6

'FORMATION - FORMATION - FORMATION!'

FORMATION FOR TODAY

In thinking about the formation of the people of God as a royal priesthood, this is inevitably influenced by the priest. Bearing this in mind it is imperative to look at the current training provision which can facilitate the formation of the priest in parish ministry, as priests are pivotal persons in the formation of the people of God.

ACCM Occasional Paper no 10 1982 deals with "The Training Of Training Incumbents". Although just over twenty years old this is still a useful paper as it gives details about the training procedure. The background of this paper is a motion carried at the July 1980 session of the General Synod which said:

> That this Synod mindful of the need to train clergy effectively for the alternative patterns of ministry applicable to the present and future, requests the Advisory Council for the Church's Ministry to bring forward proposals for "in – service" training of clergy, especially those who are training deacons, in order that all such clergy may be able to experience and be familiar with the educational methods, which will enable them to share their experience more effectively.[1]

It was mentioned in the debate of the 1980 session of General Synod that ACCM had already produced proposals for the general in-service training of clergy in the report, "The Continuing Education of the Church's Ministers" (GS MISC 122 - Para 21: Appendix B). The reported noted that:

> Becoming a training incumbent requires sensitivities and skills not necessarily acquired in other forms of ministry [2]

This report also alludes to the selection and appointment of suitable training incumbents, and points out that the appointment of the curate to the appropriate trainer are two matters of prime importance. It refers to the code of procedure for placing Deacons which states, "The over-riding consideration should be the ordinand's need for training, not the priest's need for staff."[3] The report continues to mention the criteria by which an incumbent's suitability as a trainer is assessed, and while it acknowledges that it is impossible to identify a "model" teaching incumbent since there is scope for a variety of individual gifts, there are some common factors which can be identified. In this report the following questions are raised as an indication of the suitability of a training incumbent.

> Is he theologically acute enough to be able to help the assistant, in the process of integrating his theological studies with his ministerial experience? Is he prepared still to learn himself, particularly if necessary to undergo in-service training?
> Is he able to share ministry with a colleague, including sharing difficulties as well as successes?

Is he capable of allowing an assistant to develop in
ways different from himself?
Is he able to effectively mobilize the available
resources for training the assistant?
Has he the time to devote to regular sessions for
reflection with the assistant?
Is the pattern of staff meetings and daily worship
appropriate for the assistant?[4]

The report continues to acknowledge that even with the
careful selection of training incumbents, there will still be a
need to provide them with opportunities to reflect on the
training relationship.[5] It is one thing however for this report to
have good intentions and make excellent recommendations
about training incumbents. It is altogether quite another issue
to ensure they are implemented by each diocese. Perhaps the
Church of England should consider appointing two National
Training Officers, one based at Lambeth and one at York, to
ensure that consistency in practice and standards are being
achieved by all involved in the training procedure.

Despite the specific recommendations in this report, Dr. Neil
Burgess in an account of a survey he conducted in the mid
1990's with twenty anonymous curates, raises question marks
about the suitability of many training incumbents and the
quality of training curates receive. His research leads him to
conclude that in twenty years time things will not have
changed, unless those who have power in the Church decide to
do something about it.[6]

From his research one of the main concerns he raises is that
the criteria for selecting training incumbents is often based

upon vague criteria and generalized expectations, and even when certain ministerial skills are stated these are rarely defined in ways which can measured. Training incumbents are presumed to have certain skills and aptitudes based on how long they have been ordained.[7]   While he acknowledges there are some good and a few excellent training incumbents, he identifies problems at a basic level. There are for example, incumbents who do not make time to talk to their colleagues and do not plan what they should be doing; ask how their curates are getting on or even assess their progress or future training needs. Some simply lack the educational skills to carry out a training programme.[8]   In his concluding chapter, Dr. Burgess also highlights that from his survey of twenty curates the majority reported they had no effective working relationship with their incumbent, as they were too busy and lacked the personal organizational skills to devote time for discussion and training and that in fact many were training incumbents in name only.[9]

Dr. Burgess' research reflects that over the years, the training procedure in practice has not included any real sense of accountability by the training incumbent; and it appears that dioceses have not addressed this situation. In effect many clergy work pretty much as "lone rangers" even if they are trainers, and as a result we can end up with a "cycle of deprivation" in the training procedure which deprives curates of a satisfactory training. This "cycle of deprivation" may disturbingly be repeated by future training incumbents and often reflects the inadequate training they received.

A long-term solution is for each diocese to begin to identify potential training incumbents, amongst those training as curates in the 21st Century. Dioceses can then ensure they are trained to the highest standard possible, so that in due course they are designated as training incumbents themselves and in time replace those whose who are unsuitable. This can contribute to breaking the "cycle of deprivation" where it exists in the training procedure.

Ironically ACCM paper 10 on "The Training of Training Incumbents", also states that a curate's first experience in their post after leaving theological college, is generally agreed to be of vital importance for their subsequent ministry. It continues to highlight that the parish is the context in which to build on the lessons learnt during their time of training, especially in the three main areas of pre-ordination training. These areas are identified as "academic", "pastoral" and "spiritual", and it succinctly sums up the aims of a training post which is to develop these skills. This paper also states that in the parish an integration of "theory and practice", "of theology and the experience of ministry" can now be forged which will then set the pattern for the person's future ministry.[10]

This report acknowledges that if this development is to take place continued support, encouragement and supervision will be required and a variety of people may be involved in this, although for most curates the most important single influence will be their training incumbent. It also mentions that to provide the appropriate support for a curate the training incumbent will require very considerable skills in personal relations, in theological reflection and in the educational skills mentioned in the General Synod motions.[11] Unfortunately in reality the practice of training incumbents does not necessarily or consistently match up to the recommendations expected of them.

There is one other important provision which is relevant to the training procedure of curates in the parish. This is post ordination training, appropriately and amusingly referred to as "potty training"! This continues throughout a first curacy and involves a number of curates meeting together with a parish priest, to discuss and reflect on different areas of parish ministry around once every two months This is increasingly known as (CME 1-4), Continuing Ministerial Education in the first four years of a curacy. ABM Ministry Paper No 17 January 1998: "Beginning Public Ministry" - guidelines for ministerial formation and personal development for the first four years after ordination, explains this training provision.

This ministry paper highlights the expectations which curates should aim to have as part of their training, and is a helpful guideline for the necessary areas of ministry to be covered in a title post. To help the transition from theological college to the parish it is recommended that a curate's report from his/her college should be forwarded to the CME/POT Officer, so that there can be continuity of professional and ministerial development.[12]   This paper also mentions that for these recommendations to be carried out, this would require significant changes in current practice and in the understanding of the roles of training incumbents, diocesan CME Officers and dioceses. It is envisaged that the role of the incumbent would not be seen as master to apprentice but rather as facilitator and supporter. Moreover the training incumbent needs to be trained for these tasks, including the supervisory nature of this role.[13] However the report does not state what provision is to be made to ensure these recommendations are implemented.

If this structure of training incumbents and their ongoing training, "potty training" and the implementation of CME 1 - 4 by the training officer all functioned to their maximum potential, then we would have a reasonably good system in place. Unfortunately taking into account the perennial "horror stories" people hear about (which usually involve difficulties in the relationship between the vicar and curate), the experience of the curates in Dr. Burgess' research and my personal experience; this indicates that there can be a vast gulf between the training procedure in principle and in practice. This highlights there can be a number of reasons why the training procedure may not function as efficiently and effectively as it should. For example, this can result from a lack of care and a lack of professionalism. Conflicting expectations about the nature of a curacy. Failure by the diocese to ensure the training requirements are carried out. A lack of evaluation and monitoring of a curacy, or being placed with a poor or an unsuitable training incumbent.

Dr. Burgess from his interviews with twenty curates identifies the disconcerting evidence that at times DDO's and bishops, may actually conceal evidence about training incumbents, from ordinands looking at curacies. He cites the case where one curate said:

> The DDO working with one of the bishops, had clearly put some thought in (to the appointment!); but having said that, subsequently the DDO said to me, "Well we know it's difficult there: there have been problems..."[14]

He also quotes another curate who said:

> I think I was told a lot of garbage by the bishop about the parish.....like "The vicar is the best training incumbent we have in the diocese".Well the last time I went to see (the bishop) he said, "How are things with....then? Are you still on speaking terms?" I gave a very wishy – washy answer.....and he said, "Well I couldn't work with him you know."[15]

Unfortunately my personal experience also verifies the possibility of a similar scenario happening. On the 28th June 1988 after my ordination as a deacon the Director of Training came up to me and said, "If you have any problems get in touch with me". In a brief conversation he repeated this twice. He obviously knew something I didn't but didn't clarify this unexpected warning. Without going into details and with a view to being discreet, the diocese evaluated my situation and eventually decided to move me and this happened after fourteen months. We were moved to another incumbent who also had no prior experience of training curates. As he hadn't been there long I suspect the only reason we were moved there was the convenience of an empty curate's house. I resigned after seven months. The diocese then appointed another curate after me but had to move him as they concluded the vicar was also an unsuitable training incumbent. I had the impression that in my official report the diocese made it appear that what happened reflected badly on me. This neatly deflected any criticism away from them and the way they handled my situation. A rather disingenuous achievement.

THE HIND REPORT

FORMATION FOR THE FUTURE

In July 2003, The Ministry Division of The Archbishop's Council published the report of a working party set up by the Archbishop's Council called: "FORMATION FOR MINISTRY WITHIN A LEARNING CHURCH" - The structure and funding of ordination training. The summary of this report informs us that in March 2000 the Archbishop's Council set up a review of the structure and funding of ordination training, to be chaired by the Bishop of Chichester, John Hind.[16] It also points out that the Hind report has been produced through three rounds of consultation with the Archbishop's Council, the House of Bishops, dioceses, theological colleges, courses and OLM schemes, ecumenical partners and institutions of higher education, and with the deliberations of the working party itself.[17] This report was commended to the General Synod for debate in July 2003. In Appendix 2 of the Hind report there is a list of everyone consulted which also includes lay people. In total 305 bodies or people were contacted during three consultations, although on consultation only 35 responded to the final draft of the report.[18] In my perception the summary of the Hind report fails to capture the essence of the comprehensive report, which advocates a justifiable concern with the education, formation, learning and training of ministers and the standards they attain.

On reading the Hind report it was clear that implementing the recommendation for Regional Training Partnerships, which involve the Church's various ministerial and training institutions working together collaboratively, may well prove to be a considerable challenge. This is because coordinating the resources of these different institutions, to make them available to the wider church will obviously involve increasing their workload administratively and practically. However I believe that the core concern of this report to improve the initial and ongoing ministerial education, formation and training of the clergy and the educational and theological provision for the laity, is to be warmly welcomed and wholeheartedly embraced by the Church. The proposals concerning the Regional Training Partnerships raises a concern that the foreseeable administrative, bureaucratic and institutional difficulties in implementing these proposals, may overshadow the clearly commendable recommendations concerning the ongoing education, formation and training of clergy within the context of the whole people of God.

   The summary of the Hind report states the starting point for considering models for new institutional arrangements, was the Church of England's total resources in the area of training for ministry and for lay discipleship. This was with a view to addressing other forms of adult learning in the Church, such as Reader training and other lay ministries and formal lay theological education. It is envisaged the model of Regional Training Partnerships based on eight regions would best serve the needs of the Church.[19] The Hind report informs us, "Defining the regions for a Church wide system of Regional Theological Training Partnerships is in itself an important and sensitive task, not to be undertaken lightly and without further consultation with dioceses. Before this detailed work is done there needs to be a decision in principle that the regional option is confirmed as the preferred and approved option. The working party on this report propose that if their final report is accepted by the

Archbishop's Council, the House of Bishops and the General Synod, then an appropriate body could be asked to do this further piece of work in consultation with dioceses, other churches and training institutions."[20]

A BETTER TRAINED CLERGY

The Hind report highlights the existence of a fault line, which has been discovered through their consultations with institutions and other people, between the pre-ordination training of clergy and Continuing Ministerial Education in the parish, as there is little visible connection between the training offered before and after ordination. This is because there is too much pressure on initial ministerial education to deliver everything, as well as the danger of candidates thinking their training has ended once they are ordained. Consequently the report raises the question whether the Church could develop a framework within which ministerial education is clearly seen to begin in a substantial way in pre-ordination training, and continue in a structured and related way after ordination.[21]

The report emphasises the importance of life long learning and the need for a deeper and more extended ministerial education, and voices its concern that Continuing Ministerial Education 1-4 can easily be seen to be of marginal importance in contrast to the "real" training, which is seen to take place either in the pre-ordination period or in the parish.[22] The report notes the provision for continued learning in the earliest years of ministry is uneven across the dioceses, and as a result the Church is sending mixed messages about the importance of continued learning and ministerial development. It also points out that in a few dioceses there are certified forms of study through which curates can work towards an MA in ministerial studies.[23]

The Hind report makes a number of recommendations and proposal 1 states:

> We recommend that initial, ministerial education be configured as the period of entry into training to the end of the first training post.

On one level this proposal merely formalizes the current convention that the training offered to candidates is a combination of training before ordination, apprenticeship with a training incumbent and CME 1-4. However this proposal provides an agreement to make this a reality that is visible to and acknowledged by all involved.[24] In effect the report also suggests that curates take on board that their initial formation in ministry, is a stimulus to life long learning. One of the recommendations under this proposal, is for the recently ordained minister to have an agreed allocation of time for continuing studies and reflection.With the expectation that a curate would devote a day in each working week, or its equivalent (to allow for blocks of study and reflection).[25]

In chapter five: "NEW FRAMEWORK FOR MINISTERIAL EDUCATION", in the introduction the Hind report reiterates the fact, it has "argued that a learning Church is one that promotes a dynamic and reflective discipleship for all members of the community"- and in this context the report makes its second proposal. Proposal 2 states:

We recommend that the current Bishop's regulation for training be replaced by a framework for ministerial education based on:

1/ Agreed phases of development in a formational journey, which are marked by specific levels of achievement in ministerial education, from initial exploration of vocation, via entry into training, ordination itself, title post and on into ministry:

2/ A statement of expectations for ministerial education that would indicate the qualities and learning expected of candidates at the important "thresholds" of entry into training, ordination and further phases of ministry or appointment to a post of responsibility.[26]

The report elucidates that each phase of development involves attainment in three ministerial, vocational and educational strands in preparation for movement into the next phase and it is pointed out that a candidate may be at different levels in each of these stages. It is envisaged this framework will allow theological education and training to be designed as an integrated process, enabling the fault line between IME and CME to be overcome.[27] The report clarifies that a framework of ministerial education is one which maps out a formational journey and is a means of underpinning the character and identity of the ordained minister. Although the emphasis may seem somewhat personalized as it focuses on the minister, this focus has a wider context to enable the ordained minister to serve the Church and engage in forms of education, formation and training which exploit the rich resource of a learning Church.[28]

In advocating a vision of training which is also available for lay discipleship, it may well be a wise policy for each church to consider setting up their own resource library. Each church could set aside an annual budget to build up a theological library for the benefit of the laity. Equally every candidate training for the ordained ministry should be advised to build up their own resource library and every church which has a curate can also consider giving a generous book allowance to them. Especially when the ordained minister has a family as this will limit his/her ability to purchase books.

Concerning the standards of attainment by the clergy the Hind report in proposal 4 states:

1/   Candidates for ordained ministry should have successfully achieved a minimum of diploma level in ministerial theology and practice before ordination:

2/   They continue with further learning at an agreed level according to their ability in the post ordination phase of IME:

3/   Typically, those who are to hold posts of responsibility for example team vicars, (some chaplains or incumbents) achieve a minimum of degree level in ministerial theology and practice, or its equivalent, by the time of appointment to a post of responsibility. The way this would be achieved is by recognition of a candidate having worked their way through phases of development and having achieved appropriate credits along the way.[29]

When the Hind report was discussed at the July Synod, Dr. Ian Paul tabled an amendment to drop the degree level of insistence of the working party for a curate progressing to a position of responsibility and this succeeded by 207 votes to 149. Professor Anthony Thistleton also secured the concession that alternative sources of funding should be sought, to achieve a less drastic reduction of residential places at theological colleges than the 75 identified. The Rt. Rev. John Gladwin, Bishop of Guildford and chairman of the training division of the Church of England, promised that an implementation group would progress step-by-step and ensure there was funding to keep all theological colleges open. The motion that the Synod approved the proposals set out in the report, as amended by eight amendments concerning the detail of the proposals, was carried.

THE FORMATION OF THE CURATE

Many things either negatively or positively, consciously or subconsciously may affect a curate's formation especially influential events and people from the past, present or the future. Formation is the process through which the Lord moulds the priest as he/she serves Him, and this process of transformation can result in fulfilling their potential as a priest and private person. Integrating these two areas requires suitable people to help the curate in this process of formation. Whether for example they are a spiritual director, lecturer, tutor, mentor, vicar, or a Pastoral Care & Formation Consultant: the important thing is that they are people who are able to contribute to a priest's formation through their care, encouragement, gifts, guidance, prayer, support, time and wisdom gleaned through their experience of parish ministry; or from a relevant field of expertise or their experience of church life.

Formation is a very broad process and a life-long pilgrimage. This inevitably means that a vast landscape of formation lies ahead of every curate entering ministry as a parish priest. This life-long journey embraces for example, the spiritual:

intellectual: experiential: psychological: emotional: relational: familial: pastoral: liturgical: sacramental: prayerful: biblical: theological and Christological areas of formation in the life of a priest. Formation in these diverse and at times complex areas, along with the integration of the priestly and private aspects of a minister's life should not be left to chance, in what might turn out to be a somewhat fortuitous and haphazard training experience. My vision for Pastoral Care & Formation Consultants allows them to contribute to the ongoing formation and training of curates in the parish, to enable their future ministry to have solid foundations and ministerial, professional, relational, and spiritual depth and substance. Through this process of formation the Trinity can breathe their creative life and transforming power, into and through a priest's life and ministry.

The Hind report has some helpful insights about this process of formation in the early years of a curate's ministry. It refers to this as a process that shapes the whole person, which involves growth and change and incorporates patterns of learning, piety and competence which will encourage a desire for continued growth.[30] The report highlights that formation is more than a process of moulding and involves being conformed to the pattern of Christ and his ministry. It cannot therefore be separated from the call to sacrifice and the cross that are implied in Christ's call to "Follow me". Furthermore formation should be seen as the overarching concept that integrates the person, understanding and competence.[31]

While it may seem an obvious thing for any priest to do, one of the questions to ask in their formation as they are involved in ministry, and especially when they encounter any particular difficulty is: "What is the Lord teaching me and how might He desire to shape and transform me through this; or how might this contribute to being a learning curve in my growth in ministry?" The formative element this can bring to ministry is that it helps a person to focus on what they can potentially learn, rather than become unreflective about the unrelenting demands of ministry.

The foundations of this pilgrimage in a curate's formation, could begin when a person explores their call to the ordained ministry in their home diocese. The Diocesan Director of Ordinands in consultation with this person's vicar, can build up an accurate picture of their Christian background and spirituality. As their call to ministry is tested they can be encouraged to keep a journal of formation mapping their piglrimmage and this can chart the different phases of growth towards their Selection Conference. The process of exploring a person's call to ministry, can for example, take into account a person's knowledge of the Old and New Testaments, along with their knowledge of the history and spirituality of Anglicanism. This can also include exploring their understanding of doctrine, their background in the Anglican Church and the scope of their Christian reading; along with identifying areas of personal growth whether in prayer, in ministry or in other areas of their lives. This can help to establish a discipline of planned growth which can be continued at theological college and after a person is ordained. Laying this foundation can enable a prospective curate to comprehend the thoroughness of the selection procedure, and help them to appreciate the depth and potential in candidates which the selectors are looking for.

Part of a person's formation in their diocese could include the areas which the Selectors focus on at a Selection Conference, which ABM policy paper 3A 1993 reminds us of. A synopsis of these is found in Appendix A.[32]

 * Ministry within the Church of England
 * Vocation   * Faith   * Spirituality
 * Personality and Character   * Relationships
 * Leadership and Collaboration   * Quality of Mind

As a potential curate-priest embarks on this pilgrimage of formation, areas which might be perceived as possible weaknesses, can also be identified and explored as potential areas of growth. Taking the first tentative step on this journey at the early stage of a person's call in their home diocese, allows him/her to lay the foundations for this invaluable process which can facilitate change, growth and transformation and ultimately maturity as a priest and a private person.

PASTORAL CARE & FORMATION CONSULTANTS

Bearing in mind the current proposals of the Hind report are not expected to be fully implemented until 2008 and despite the current training procedure, there is still a high element of risk involved in whether a curate receives a comprehensive and first class training in the parish. Consequently I believe it is time for the Church of England to address the fortuitous and inconsistent nature, of how the current training procedure in practice often turns out. This unsatisfactory situation may well prevent many curates from laying solid foundations in all areas of parish ministry, which they can subsequently build on in the future and in turn this can stunt their growth and formation in ministry.

In the Autumn of 1999 I had a vision for Pastoral Care & Formation Consultants, which I believe can make an important contribution to the training and formation or curates in parish ministry. I believe this vision reflects God's concern for the way curates are trained and nurtured in the Church of England. This can be implemented in two ways. Each diocese can appoint a stipendiary Consultant or one on a voluntary basis. This vision allows someone outside the parish to be involved in a curate's training by seeing them once a month for a morning or afternoon, to objectively contribute to their formation as a minister and parish priest. Having a Consultant would be to the advantage of the training incumbent with the innumerable demands on his/her time, and this would also benefit the congregation as the quality of ministry they receive from the curate should be enhanced. This would also be a significant advantage to a curate as it involves having a Consultant experienced in parish ministry, who takes a personal interest in their development and formation in an objective way.

As there is often an idealism and an innocence about going into ministry, this may well leave many curates regardless of their age, vulnerable to the devouring nature of parish ministry. A call to the ordained ministry is also a call to an increasingly complex profession and without sounding patronizing and acknowledging all they have to offer, curates are a precious commodity who require careful nurture. An outside Consultant can help to nurture, protect and support them as they adapt to parish ministry. The aspect of pastoral care for curates is a very significant one, and there may well be no meaningful support in this area from the training incumbent. From the recent research of Dr. Yvonne Warren, she discovered the pastoral care of clergy appears to be very unstructured and can result in a lack of support for them throughout their ministry.[33] In this area a Consultant can advise and help a curate to set up a support system, which can provide pastoral care for him/her, their spouse and family.

Dioceses with a large number of curates can appoint a full time Pastoral Care & Formation Consultant, while others which do not have so many curates can make this a half time appointment, combined with a half time parish post. While it is envisaged that a Consultant would meet up with each curate once a month for either a morning or afternoon to reflect on and discuss the training procedure, where this is not possible the Consultant may recruit other suitable people to act in the same capacity. For example other excellent parish priests or suitable retired clergy can be recruited. As an alternative to employing a full time Consultant each diocese can appoint suitable people in a voluntary capacity. This can involve existing parish priests considered to be excellent role models, or retired priests regarded in the same light, or other people who have considerable experience of parish ministry.

Without detracting from the contribution of training incumbents, or POT/CME officers, having an outside Consultant a curate sees on a regular basis, can be a safe and objective environment in which to voice any concern or question about ministry. This is especially true, when for example, a curate may wish to question the prevailing practice of the incumbent, which might be perceived as a threat and which it may well not be prudent or diplomatic to raise. Alternatively a curate may wish to discuss aspects of ministry that are causing difficulty or which he/she feels vulnerable about, and which it would be preferable not to raise with their incumbent. Equally it is quite likely that a keen and inquisitive curate, will have many difficult questions to raise about practice, in areas of ministry or theology which their incumbent may have never deeply explored.   The reason an outside Consultant can embrace such searching questions, is because they have acquired an "inhabited wisdom" about parish ministry and are not personally threatened by these things.

This ties in with the guiding principle for ministerial education which the Hind report espouses.   "Theological education needs a clear conception of its distinctive thrust – its goal...The goal I think is an inhabited Wisdom (immersed in scripture, the continuity of the Church's life in God, and in a Spirit-informed reason) in the Church, one that is active in responding to the issues of present day life.   This definition brings together the theological, formational and practical dimensions of training."[34]   A Consultant should ideally be someone who personifies this "inhabited wisdom."

Consultants aim to contribute to the development of ministerial gifts, spirituality and to encourage professional excellence.   They would also contribute to curates laying solid foundations in all areas of parish ministry, and would also provide pastoral care and support for the curate and facilitate this on a wider basis where necessary.   The primary brief of a Consultant would be to "SERVE" curates in their formation and training as leaders and priests, so that they obtain the maximum benefit, learning and training from their first curacy.   A Consultant would be able to give a curate the opportunity to discuss and reflect on any issues about parish ministry in complete confidentiality. This would also give a curate the opportunity to share about any other concerns in his/her personal life in complete confidentiality too. When the Consultant meets up with the curate once a month for a morning or afternoon, they can agree to spend some time on specific areas of ministry every three months, or focus on phases of accomplishments which the Hind report recommends (when they are implemented); as well as to focus on specific issues the curate raises.

While there are undoubtedly some good training incumbents, I believe there is still a level of fortuitousness and inconsistency about the quality of training a curate may receive. Alongside this there are the perennial "horror stories" about the vicar-curate relationship which a Consultant can objectively advice a curate about, when he/she is experiencing difficulties in this area. Consultants also aim to ensure, that a curate's training does not get hijacked by the relentless demands of parish ministry or by the unrelenting schedule of a busy training incumbent, who may not have adequate time to devote to the training procedure.

When a curate finds they are in an difficult training parish, having an outside Consultant ensures that someone is already in place to immediately intercept such a potentially damaging situation. The Consultant can help a curate to work through the presenting difficulties and ensure that he/she still learns as much as is possible from their curacy. Consultants can also help curates not to needlessly trip up over themselves, through any lack of wisdom in dealing with people and situations in the parish, by facilitating a greater level of self awareness, and an awareness of the issues and human nature which these situations involve. A Consultant would also bring greater confidence to a curate's training as the direction and outcome of their curacy is no longer largely dependent on the incumbent. Consequently it would also bring a greater measure of control to a curate's learning, formation and training.

THE FORMATION OF A TRAINING INCUMBENT

While ACCM paper 10 1982 on the "Training Of Training Incumbents" is a reassuring document, it is still nevertheless not as comprehensive as it might be in identifying more of the suitable qualities in a prospective trainer. I believe it is helpful to identify more of these qualities in a profile of a training incumbent. However this is not advocating perfection or that he/she is a spiritual superman/woman. This profile could focus on four areas of formation: "professional qualities", "spiritual qualities", "relational qualities" and "personal qualities." What this profile points to is that these qualities can be identified as the benchmark by which to assess whether someone is a suitable trainer, and can also indicate any areas for ongoing education, formation and training for existing training incumbents. The danger in such a comprehensive profile is having expectations which are far too high. Although of course it is possible to expect too little. However aiming at the highest standards is more likely to encourage a higher level of excellence. It is in the pursuit of this excellence that the following profile is suggested as a guideline, along with the recommendation that these incumbents are encouraged to think in terms of their ongoing formation as trainers. Something which has to be continually reflected upon and evaluated, to ensure they are setting themselves aims to continue to grow professionally.

PROFESSIONAL QUALITIES

The incumbent is recognized as an excellent parish priest and is ideally experienced in training curates. He/she has been identified as a good role model for curates to learn from and work with and is also acknowledged as a very competent leader, pastor and preacher, who knows their strengths and weaknesses. Alongside this he/she will also have a very high standard of liturgical skill and be highly competent in leading both traditional and contemporary worship. The incumbent consistently aims to integrate "theory and practice" and "theology and experience" in parish ministry, and takes the issue of their ongoing training seriously; and seeks to be up to date with the educational, supervisory and training skills available in the diocese and wider Church. He/she can reflect theologically and is open to feedback and evaluation from the people of God. The incumbent has a good understanding of human nature and of volunteers in the church and what makes them tick, as well as understanding curates and what motivates them too. He/she also aims to work collaboratively with the people of God, and is keen to help them discover and develop their particular gifts within the body of Christ. The incumbent also keeps up to date with current publications, valuing them as an indispensable resource in ministry.

The training incumbent willingly takes responsibility for the welfare of their curate and family and takes a genuine interest in them. He/she also sees it as their responsibility to ensure the curate's training is progressing in a satisfactory manner, and understands that the development and formation of their curate's ministry in the formative years is absolutely vital. The incumbent also willingly gives the commitment and time which having a curate inevitably involves and sees their role as a trainer, as primarily the privilege of serving.

SPIRITUAL QUALITIES

A training incumbent is chosen because he/she has spiritual depth and substance, and is committed to a discipline of prayer both privately and corporately, as well as being devoted to the study of scripture. He/she seeks to maintain a living relationship with God, Christ and the Holy Spirit and makes it a priority in parish ministry to nurture their love for the Trinity. Something which they acknowledge is a response to the initiative of the Trinity in their lives, as they realize that these Trinitarian relationships are the springboard from which all aspects of ministry depend and flow. Therefore an incumbent's ministry is characterized and motivated by seeking to point people to the Lord and helping them develop and nurture their own relationship with the Trinity. He/she is also appreciative of and open to learning from other traditions within the Church of England, and does not have a siege mentality which narrowly defends their own particular churchmanship.

The incumbent nurtures an interest in mission and is keen to encourage the people of God to take an active interest in evangelism too. He/she has also learnt that ministry is a pilgrimage of faith and obedience and seeks to encourage the people of God in this journey too. Integral to the incumbent's walk of faith is learning to listen to the Lord speaking to the Church through the Scriptures, and encouraging the people of God to cultivate this gift too. An incumbent seeks to bless their curate and the people of God in prayer and through the words he/she speaks in private and in public. He/she will bless them in the name of the Lord and bless their gifts and ministries and all they give to the Lord in serving Him.

RELATIONAL QUALITIES

A training incumbent is acknowledged to have good inter personal skills especially in relating to curates, and is a person who has developed the art of diplomacy in dealing with the diversity of volunteers in the Church. A vicar looks to be affirming, encouraging, helpful and supportive to their curate and is aware of the importance of not speaking any negative words about him/her to other members of the fellowship, knowing this is unchristian and unprofessional. Qualities which are indispensable in establishing a relationship of affection and trust with their curate.

A training incumbent always looks to be absolutely loyal to their curate especially when members of the congregation criticize him/her behind his back. Occasionally this criticism may be justified and can be a learning point, but the vicar can usually tell the difference between what is objectively helpful and what is plainly uncharitable. He/she knows it is not necessary to bolster their own self esteem at the expense of being disloyal to the curate. An incumbent will also stand up for and defend their curate in private and in public, knowing that this cements and nurtures their relationship and fosters trust and respect.

PERSONAL QUALITIES

Michael Green in his autobiography "Adventure of Faith", mentions two qualities which he particularly valued in his training vicar. He says, "He treated Rosemary and me like extra children of his own and gave us a marvelous start. We felt loved and wanted. I believe it is important for a young curate to go to a place where their incumbent loves him or her, than to go to a place that prides itself on being "sound".[35] He also adds, "….Those were some of the areas of ministry I discovered under the guidance of a loving vicar who rejoiced in any small successes that came my way, far more than he did in his own."[36] Here Michael touches on vitally important issues in a curate's training and formation, as he/she looks to their vicar to gladly and lovingly embraces him/her and their family. The curate also looks to their vicar to rejoice in his/her gifts rather than one who is silently envious and cannot find it in their heart to rejoice with their colleague, when the Lord obviously works through them.

A curate also looks to their vicar to be a person who is secure and not easily threatened or jealous of him/her, or of their ministry or popularity, or of peoples' appreciation when it comes. When a training incumbent has not embraced their security in God they are virtually certain to compete against their curate. This immature competitiveness will continually undermine their curate and it will also adversely affect his/her confidence, formation and progress in ministry. The training incumbent will then have to relate to their curate on a surface level which will inevitably lack integrity or relational depth, as this competitive spirit will constantly seek to bolster their own fragile ego.

A training incumbent openly and unreservedly extends the hand of fellowship and friendship to their curate and family. He/she is a trustworthy person who is caring, thoughtful, and who understands how much there is for the curate to learn and how many adjustments have to be made in the transition to parish life. The incumbent also has a good level of self awareness and as an individual is open intellectually and spiritually, as well as receptive to the gifts a new curate brings.

FOUNDATIONAL ATTITUDES IN A CURATE

There are eight qualities beginning with "L" which I believe it is wise for a curate to take to their new parish, as an integral part of their formation when they are ordained. The first quality is highlighted by wearing an imaginary "L" plate, which is a reminder that primarily a curate is a "LEARNER" and this is their apprenticeship in parish ministry. My perception is that the overwhelming majority of curates automatically think of themselves as leaders who are going to play a significant leadership role, which along the way they may do. However there is nothing as contradictory as a conceited curate, who comes with a supposed expertise or excellence in ministry and thinks he/she already knows all there is about parish ministry.

Another indispensable quality for a curate is to be a channel through whom the "LOVE" of Christ is shared with the people of God. Learning to love the different personalities in the congregation and the people who are demanding and difficult, is an important process in the formation of a curate's ministry. Alongside this indispensable quality is for a curate to nurture their "LOVE" for the Lord. In reality this is learning to respond to the overtures of love which God, Christ and the Spirit initiate in their life. This is also an important part in the formation of a curate because it will be an influential factor in their ministry. On occasions Christians and parish life will inevitably stretch this love to the limit.

Another important quality which a curate would be advised to bring to a new parish is "LOYALTY" to their vicar, because there will always be people who criticize the vicar in front of the curate. Here he/she has to avoid courting popularity with the parishioners at the vicar's expense, because sooner or later this will surface and it will also have a very detrimental impact on their relationship. The easiest way to remain loyal is to tell anyone who complains, to go and speak to vicar and tell him/her all about it!

Another relevant quality for a curate to take to the new parish is that of "LOOKING" to point people to the Lord. That does not mean a curate cannot be themselves and it also doesn't mean he/she cannot enjoy praise which comes their way. But what it does involve is their motivation in ministry. Is the curate's primary concern to point people to the Lord or to him/herself? Another necessary quality a curate should seek to cultivate is to be a "LISTENER" and to take a real interest in people, as this helps to get to know them on a meaningful level and establishes a rapport and trust with them. People are always pleased to have a minister take an interest in their lives. Listening is also beneficial to the priest as it can help his/her preaching to be more pastorally relevant.

Another vital quality that a curate should bring to a parish and which hopefully will have been cultivated at theological college, is "LAYING" good foundations of self awareness. For example this may involve learning what his/her temperamental traits are, or this may involve cultivating a good self awareness of strengths and weaknesses in ministry, or being aware how he/she comes across to other people.

The last quality I would recommend a curate takes to a new parish, is "LOWLINESS". A model of Christ like humility tempered by modesty. For whether a curate realizes it or not he/she has far more to learn, than can possibly be imagined on first entering parish ministry. Humility keeps a curate in touch with their learning potential, whereas conceit invariably means not learning and standing still for years on end, without realizing it.

I am aware of the danger that at times clergy can take themselves too seriously. On occasions a sense of humour and being laid back, can be a helpful quality for the incumbent and curate in helping to counteract this tendency. Bearing this in mind an excerpt by John Betjeman is included. I hope this in not considered too inappropriate in making this point!

> When things go wrong it's rather tame
> To find we are ourselves to blame,
> It gets the trouble over quicker
> To go and blame things on the vicar.
> The vicar after all is paid
> To keep us bright and undismayed.

Dear people who have read so far
I know how kind you really are,
I hope you are always seeing
Your vicar as a human being
Making allowances when he
Does things with which you don't agree.[37]

Here I am inclined to think that the clergy might mischievously re-write these few lines so they read.

When things go wrong it's rather tame
To find the clergy are to blame,
It gets the trouble over quicker
To go and blame things on the laity.
The laity after all are volunteers
Who should be bright and undismayed!

Dear clergy who have read so far
I know how kind you really are,
I hope you're always seeing
The laity as human beings,
Making allowances when they often
Do things with which you don't agree!

FORMATION IN THE FIRST FOUR YEARS

There is a publication by the Advisory Board Of Ministry called "Beginning Public Ministry" - guidelines for ministerial formation and personal development for the first four years after ordination: ABM Ministry paper No 17 January 1998.

This is a helpful guide for curates going to their first parish. The introduction highlights the polarized perceptions which parishioners and curates may have, of their respective expectations about what a curate should do. These may range from a lack of understanding about the purpose of a first curacy by parishioners, to the curate's impatience to "get on with the job".[38]   This report also highlights the necessity of understanding the nature of a curacy. Having access to this can prevent ordinands leaving theological college thinking their training is complete, when in reality the overwhelming majority of their practical experience is about to begin. A curate looking through this report prior to arriving in the parish may well remove a potential minefield of misunderstanding, about the nature and purpose of a first curacy.

This report also highlights that parishes welcoming a new incumbent who has just only served a first curacy, expect him/her to possess certain technical skills and mentions that some clergy felt inadequately prepared to exercise certain aspects of public ministry.[39] It also recognizes with the increasing move towards collaborative ministry, that the training role of the incumbent was becoming that of a coach or learning facilitator.[40] It may well be advisable to recommend that the incumbent sees his role as an enabler, which introduces more of an element of equality in the relationship.

THE ISSUE OF AUTHORITY

This report raises the issue of expectations to be met during the first years of a curacy and some are worth highlighting as they are extremely important. The curate is expected to have a working understanding of issues of authority both delegated and assigned under canon law, in the practice of ordained ministry and parish life, including registers, faculties etc.[41] I believe the issue of submitting to the authority of the incumbent, is an extremely important one for a curate to explore prior to arriving in the parish, as the vicar and curate have to relate to one another in a variety of roles within their working relationship. These roles may well cause a great deal of frustration and difficulty, especially if the curate has not thought through the implication of submitting to the incumbent's authority.

For example the vicar and curate may relate to each other as colleagues working together: on a fellowship level as Christians: on a friendship level: on the level of trainer and learner: on a social level: on a leadership level and on the level of one having authority and the other being under it. At times having to juggle this variety of inter changeable roles can be difficult and complex, especially for the curate. This can be further complicated because many of the influential lay leaders or other colleagues, will already have an established and recognized authority which far exceeds that of the curate. Therefore this can turn out to be rather frustrating for the curate, depending on how he/she deals with the fact that while officially having authority, he/she may have virtually none in practice.

The issue of authority may also be further complicated by the fact a curate in his/her secular career may have been a person with a considerable degree of authority, influence and responsibility. Adapting to the realm of authority within the church and amongst volunteers, can turn out to be a major issue of contention and one which a curate often trips over as he/she tries to come to terms with this.   I believe three things can go to towards resolving this potential minefield for a curate. Firstly it is an issue which should be explored at theological college. Secondly a curate has to accept the fact that ultimately he/she is under the authority of their incumbent, despite the many different roles they both have to adopt when relating to each other. Thirdly a curate may also have to accept that in practice and in reality he/she will probably exercise very little authority, and that what has to be learnt is to become a person of influence and work within these boundaries. Taking this as an opportunity to learn how he/she might wisely use their authority as an incumbent in the future.

Three other issues are raised in ABM Ministry paper 17 1998, that are invaluable for a curate to explore during his/her first post and possibly during their theological training. The first concerns discovering their leadership style and its strengths and weaknesses, as well as understanding other styles of leadership. The second concerns being a public figure and understanding the demands and implications this brings. This is extremely important as the overwhelming majority of people will perceive the priest as a having a public role. The third concerns the curate nurturing his/her private life and developing personal friendships, as these are the areas in which a sense of belonging and identity as an individual is affirmed and authenticated. Being well grounded in his/her personal life in this way helps a curate to integrate his public and private persona.

Two other issues from this report are also worth mentioning. The first highlights that the first four years of ordained ministry are the time for immersion in a wide range of ministerial experiences, and the development of the capacity to bear the public roles and responsibilities of the ordained person. Moreover that a curate needs to be seen to be loosened from the parish to a greater extent than generally at present in order to have access to a wider base of experience.[42] Here I would recommend that once a month curates are involved in worship on a Sunday at a fellowship whose churchmanship is different from their own. This would influence their formation as Anglican parish priests and enable them to sympathise with and understand, the comprehensive nature of the spirituality of the Church of England.

I would also strongly recommend that as part of a working contract a training incumbent and curate agree on a form of evaluation. Here evaluation can include affirmation as well as recommendation. Affirmation involves highlighting the positive things about an area of ministry and recommendation involves suggesting ways of improving or growing in an area of ministry. A curate can also carry out his/her own evaluation in areas of ministry and occasionally lay people may also be invited to contribute to this process. The advantage of an agreed method of evaluation is that this allows for regular feedback, which can enable excellence in ministry to develop. This also encourages an ongoing learning process and teaches a curate and anyone else being evaluated, to be accountable to others. This helps to prevent a false and inflated sense of perception about their own ministry from forming. Where there is no regular form of evaluation, the curate runs the risk of standing still and not growing in ministry, without realizing it.

FORMATION AFTER A FIRST CURACY

There has been an increasing awareness in the Church of England in recent years about the importance of the ongoing education, formation and training of its clergy in parish life and this is represented by the publication of the Hind report. In connection with this I would recommend that a curate's second appointment should also be designated a training post, and an apprenticeship in being a vicar. In this respect each diocese could also appoint a stipendiary Pastoral Care & Formation Consultant or voluntary Consultants, to meet up with curates who become vicars. In a diocese where there are too many curates in their second post for the stipendiary Consultant to meet up with, then voluntary Consultants could be appointed as has already been recommended for first curacies.

Although it may seem somewhat optimistic to recommend at this stage, all clergy after their second post could also be linked to a Consultant to continue their ongoing education, formation and training. In principle this could transform the ongoing formation and training of clergy in the Church of England. I believe that to appoint stipendiary or voluntary Consultants will make a considerable contribution to the quality of the clergy and to the growth of the Church; in terms of her confidence, effectiveness, leadership, maturity, numerical growth, spirituality and witness.

APPENDIX 1

SELECTION CONFERENCES

It is undeniably to the advantage of anyone with a perceived call to the ordained ministry, as well as to those preparing people to go forward to a Selection Conference, to obtain the literature available about the selection procedure. There is a small booklet published by The Ministry Division of The Archbishop's Council, Church House, Great Smith Street, London SWIP 3NZ - "Going To A Selection Conference". In the introduction (no page number is given) it mentions that its purpose is to respond to some common questions about the central selection procedures of the Church of England. This introduction also mentions that there are two specific reports published by The Ministry Division about Selection Conferences, that are also available from the Church House Publications Bookshop, Church House, Great smith Street, London SWIP 3NZ. The first is particularly helpful and is indispensable to anyone preparing to go to a Selection Conference. This is ABM POLICY PAPER 3A: "The Report Of A Working Party On Criteria For Selection For Ministry In the Church of England" October 1993.

There is usually an aura of mystery about Selection Conferences, concerning the process by which candidates are either recommended to train for ministry or are turned down and rejected. This mystery is perpetuated when members of a fellowship are completely baffled why a candidate from their church, who they consider called by the Lord and suitably gifted is not recommended to train. There is no official report or reasons given to a candidate or their home church, why someone was not recommended to train. This results in an element of mystery which puzzles people as there is no information to alleviate the disappointment and often considerable pain, of understanding why a candidate was turned down. Obtaining a copy of ABM Policy Paper 3A 1993 will definitely dispel any aura of mystery surrounding Selection Conferences, as this reveals the thoroughness of the selection procedure and how it works, as well as clarifying the detailed guidelines which Selectors are given in deciding whether or not to recommend a person for training.

Before I was sponsored by the Diocese of Southwell in 1985 for a second Selection Conference I had an interview with a panel of five people, two clergy and three lay people. Their responsibility was to decide on behalf of the bishop whether to recommend me to go forward to a Selection Conference. I had already met the Diocesan Director of Ordinands on a number of occasions and had written an essay for him about being a priest. Prior to seeing the panel I identified and thought through the issues which I considered they may have asked me questions about. These evolved around potential areas of growth which had been identified with the help of a minister four years earlier, when I had not been recommended to train at my first Selection Conference. As it turned out I was asked questions around these areas and my preparation ensured that a good impression was made. It is an absolute necessity that anyone going forward for selection is seen to be a thoughtful person. Careful preparation ensures that a candidate comes across in the best possible light at interview.

Anyone going forward for selection would be strongly advised to ask their diocese to arrange at least one interview by a panel consisting of both clergy and laity, to help prepare them for their Selection Conference interviews. Anyone not very well prepared or not prepared at all for their Conference, runs an overwhelmingly high risk of not being recommended to train. Greater emphasis on candidates being more thoroughly prepared before attending a Selection Conference also helps to ensure the quality of candidates increases. ABM Policy Paper 6 1995, mentioned a fall in the number of candidates recommended to train in 1993 from 53% to 47%. This highlighted concerns about central selection. These concerns included anxiety about churchmanship bias and the number and quality of those offering themselves for ministry, and the need for more integration between dioceses and the center.[1]

A consultation with dioceses and the Bishop's Selectors also expressed concern about the low recommendation rate, which indicated a lack of correlation between local and national procedures. At the heart of this concern lie questions as to whether standards are too high and the local context not taken seriously enough.[2] This issue almost certainly revolves around how thoroughly candidates are prepared for selection by their diocese and home church, and whether a comprehensive enough level of preparation takes place. This lack of preparation, may reflect a lack of awareness at local level of the high standards required by candidates at a Selection Conference, and may also reflect a lack of awareness of the thoroughness of the selection procedure. These issues can be resolved at a stroke if candidates and their home church purchased a copy of ABM Policy Paper 3A 1993. This report is a real eye opener about the careful, thorough and professional manner of selection, in a truly "gob smacking way"! Anyone reading it is guaranteed to be struck by how demanding it is to be recommended to train for the ordained ministry.   But the "double whammy" that will flatten almost everyone, concerns the often inadequate or poor preparation for selection candidates receive.   I believe this is because their home churches are not aware of the exceptionally high standards that are expected, or how the selection procedure works in practice, and the depth of preparation advisable before anyone goes to a Selection Conference.

APPENDIX 2

THE RELATIONAL DIMENSION OF MINISTRY

Andrew Irvine mentions that "Ministry modeled on the life of Jesus is always relational."[1] He has some helpful and perceptive insights concerning the different levels of relationships that a minister is likely to be involved in. In fact he outlines the possibility of seven types of relationships a minister is likely to encounter.[2] He believes that a minister can cope with this diversity of inter-personal relationships provided that their own personhood and self is nurtured through having healthy relationships.[3] However he does not go on to say whether these meaningful relationships will be developed within a congregation or are dependent on a minister's relationships outside the church, which might involve family members, a variety of friends, spiritual director or mentor, or former secular work colleagues, or former college friends.

He raises the possibility that the majority of a minister's inter-personal relationships as a public person, may not in fact meet his/her emotional and relational needs as an individual on a deeper level. Moreover there is the risk of developing no relationships and then experiencing separation and isolation. When this happens the lack of a solid relational basis is damaging both for personal development and for the fulfillment of ministry. Ultimately he believes that one cannot be a complete being in either without meaningful relationships.[4]

This highlights the fact the minister is both a public figure and a private person and that he/she must learn to cultivate and nurture meaningful relationships, in the personal sphere of their life with people who know him/her well. Of course it is also possible that within a minister's congregation certain people may become personal friends. Although it is unlikely this will happen successfully and without problems, unless the minister takes care to establish the boundaries of trust and confidentiality within these relationships concerning church life and their personal life.

Being aware of Irvine's different types of inter personal relationships can be helpful for the minister, as often relating on these levels involves a high degree of giving to people. Understanding how these different levels of relationships work, takes away the mystery of why a minister may not be finding nurture or renewal through these relational encounters. I believe the reason is that the minister is not receiving fellowship on a deeper level of intimacy. This is where the minister's meaningful relationships from his personal circle of friends can redress this balance.

We can perceive how these different levels of relationships with people occurred in Jesus' life too, and see that he found fellowship and friendship, nurture and support from within his own private circle of personal friends, rather than from the crowds he ministered to. Crowds he was invariably always giving to as opposed to his circle of friends where there could be a giving as well as a receiving.

Andrew Irvines's seven levels of relationship have the following headings and the last two are described in detail.

* The Passing Nod   * The Courteous Exchange
* The Neighbourly Chatter   * The Working Relationship
* The Social Connection

* The Depth Interaction

"This is a very special level of relationship that develops out of a sense of trust, shared experiences and the assurance of confidentiality. It is at this level that the workings of the heart and mind are mutually shared at a consistent level. The number of persons allowed to enter this level of interaction is limited and they usually do so through trust or necessity.

*The Intimate Encounter

This is the deepest level of interaction and implies a spiritual interaction in which progressive self-revelation, allows entrance into an ever deepening sphere of relationship founded on trust which transcends all barriers. The term interaction indicates a mutually shared relationship based on equality and is reserved for the significant others in our life."[5]

I believe that understanding these different levels of relationships is indispensable in parish ministry, as it prevents both the priest and the people of God expecting their minister to have an intimate relationship with everyone in the church. Equally we do well to remember that the majority of a minister's relational encounters are usually either in the context of seeing people at church, or at meetings, or in their home. In practice this means interaction with people in short time slots. Establishing relationships with the people in this way may depend more on diplomacy and social skills, than fellowship in the Spirit.

This may come as quite a shock to ministers new to parish life who used to spend the entire day in their secular careers working with the same people, and who also used to spend most of their time every day at college with people too. In both these situations there was the opportunity to establish a rapport with work colleagues or student friends, by virtue of being with them for consistently long periods of time. In contrast as a minister the priest often works alone from home and frequently has no colleagues to work alongside.

One other writer mentions the importance of friendship as a means of growth for ministers,which is worth exploring in the context of church relationships.   Kotva Jr. mentions the importance of seeking out good friends, as friendships have the "instrumental value of being morally formative."[6] Within the framework of such friendships may be found the "primary adult context for the development of moral judgment and character", which may well be a mutual process.[7]

Kotva Jr. sees this friendship as playing an influential part in our development as individuals. Within this level of relationship we may well seek advice or expose our judgments to correction. Equally at times our friends might neither advise nor critique but simply listen attentively, in order to allow us to listen to ourselves speaking as we talk and think through important issues. Friends may also come from different backgrounds and histories and so bring a different perspective to issues that concern us.[8]   On a different level he speaks of the moral influence derived from sharing mutual interests on a companionship level. Moreover the satisfaction of simply being with one another and sharing together can affirm our mutual appreciation, which in turn can renew us and save us from burn out.[9]

Kotva Jr. also highlights another intrinsically important component of the moral significance of friendship. He quotes Paul Wadell who says:

> Some of our identity comes from our recognition of another, but a lot of it comes from how we are recognized by them. So much of who we are is a measure of the attention we have received, so much of how we think of ourselves, our appreciation of self, our self image and identity is other bestowed. It is exactly this reciprocity that makes friendship so morally important to securing identity.[10]

This profound perception highlights that the core essence of who we really are is reflected by our close friends. Such friendships help to keep ministers firmly grounded as public figures, rather than be consumed by their public persona or roles.

For a minister to be with members of their immediate or extended family, friends from their home church or within their own congregation, college friends, colleagues from their secular career, or people connected to ministry who know them really well, allows a minister to be him/herself in the sphere of their personal life. Although distance and time may make it difficult to have frequent contact with all of these people, I believe it is indispensable to nurture these important relationships. Maintaining contact with these people enables a minister to maintain links with his/her roots and helps to nurture a sense of belonging and identity with the influential people in their life, with whom he/she has meaningful relationships on a deeper level.

In relation to being both a public and a private person Alan Abernethy touches on an aspect of this which he shares from his experience. He says, "I do not have to become someone else, or to have certain theological views, or be a wonderfully skilled rector. I am called to be me".[11]   For the priest learning to be a public figure and also learning to integrate that with being oneself, is a considerable challenge. Discovering and nurturing the real self in private and within the circle of our personal friends who know us well, will ensure that our personality is not submerged nor suppressed by the fact we are a public person as a priest.

FOOTNOTES

PREFACE

1   R. C. Moberly   Ministerial Priesthood   John Murray   London 1899   244

2   ABM Ministry Paper 13 1996   Recovering Confidence
    The Call To ordained Ministry In A Changing World   30

3   T. F. Torrance   Royal Priesthood - A Theology of Ordained Ministry
    T & T Clark   1999   82

4   Ibid   87

5   R. C. Moberly   ibid   254

6   Ashley Benedict in The Theology Of Priesthood
    Editors   Goergen & Carrido   The Liturgical Press   2000   141

7   John Udris in Simple Priesthood by Sean Connolly   Paulist Press   2001   142

CHAPTER 1

1   G. Wenham   Commentary on Leviticus   Eerdmans   1979   129

2   Ibid   26

3   Ibid   27

4   P. Jensen   Sacrifice In The Bible Edited by R.T. Beckwith &
    M. J. Selman   Baker Paternoster Press 1995   36

5   Ibid   37

6   T. F. Torrance   Ibid   2-3

7   Ibid 3

8   Ibid 5

9   Ibid 5

10 Ibid 5

11 Raymond Brown Commentary on Hebrews   IVP 1982   93-94

12 Ibid 94

13 Ibid   152

14 W. Nee The Normal Christian Life   Kingsway   1989   13-14

15 R. C Moberly   ibid   245

16 Ibid   246

17 Ian Bradley   The Power of Sacrifice   DLT   1995   284

18 Ibid   285

19 Ibid   286

20 Charitie De Chenez   Before The Throne Of God Above
    Common Praise Canterbury Press   2002   261

21 Julian of Norwich Translated by Julia Bolton Holloway   DLT 2003 35

CHAPTER 2

1 M. Ramsay The Christian Priest Today SPCK 2001 109-110

2 M. Himes in Priesthood In The Modern World
Edited by Karen S. Smith Sheed & Ward 1999 46

3 Steven Croft Ministry In Three Dimensions DLT 2000 85-87 & 95

4 David Power in Priesthood In The Modern World Ibid 32

5 K. Mason Priesthood and Society Canterbury Press 2002 40

6 Ibid 7

7 R. C. Moberly Ibid 256

8 K. Mason Ibid 55

9 K. Leech Spirituality And Pastoral Care Sheldon Press 1986 130-131

10 C. Cocksworth & R. Brown Being A Priest Today Canterbury Press 2002 25

11 Arthur Middleton Towards A Renewed Priesthood Gracewing 1995 24

12 Ibid 5

13 K. Leech Soul Friend DLT 1996 30

14 Ibid 31

15 R. C. Moberly ibid 293

16 Ibid 299

17 Ibid 254

18 Ibid   254

19 Arthur Middleton   Ibid   10 - 12

20 John Twisleton   Empowering Priesthood   Tufton Books   2002   41

21 Michael Fallon   A Priest After My Own Heart   St. Pauls   2001   69

22 Kenneth Stevenson   Do This – The Shape, Style and Meaning Of
    The Eucharist   Canterbury Press 2002   88-89

23 M. Perham   New Handbook Of Pastoral Liturgy   SPCK   2000   114-115

24 Ibid   115

25 C. Cocksworth & R. Brown   Ibid   76

26 Scott Kahn   The Lamb's Supper   DLT   2003   51

27 J. Gledhill   Leading A Local Church   SPCK   2003   49

28 Ibid   49

29 K. Leech   Ibid 130-131

30 C. Cocksworth & R. Brown   Ibid   75

31 Douglas Dales   Glory – The Spiritual Theology Of Michael Ramsay
    Canterbury Press   2003   91

32 Ibid   92

33 ACCM 22 Education For The Church's Ministry 1987   28

34 Ibid   29-30

35 R. Greenwood   Transforming Priesthood   SPCK   1999   149

36 Christopher Gray   The Fire And The Clay   Guiver et al   SPCK   1999   48

37 Ibid   49

38 R. C. Moberly   Ibid   258

CHAPTER 3

1   George Herbert   Selected Poems   Everyman   1996   89

2   C. Gray   Ibid   43

3   Ibid   48

4   Kenneth Leech   Soul Friend   DLT   1996   163

5   T. Smail   The Giving Gift   DLT   1994   13

6   F. D. Bruner   A Theology Of The Holy Spirit   Eerdmans   1974   165

7   Bruner Ibid   159

8   C. Stanley   The Wonderful Spirit Filled Life   Nelson   1992   15

9   M. Volf   Exclusion And Embrace   Abingdon Press   1996   125

10 Ibid   126

11 Ibid   126

12 Ibid   128

13 Ibid   129

14 Ibid   129

15 C. Cocksworth & R.Brown   ibid   106

16 K. Leech   ibid   163

17 E. Underhill   The Ways Of The Spirit   Crossroad   1990   176

18 Ibid   178

19 M. Ramsey   ibid   14

20 Ibid   14

21 Ibid   15

CHAPTER 4

1   R. C. Moberly   Ibid   286

2   Ibid   285

3   Ibid   289

4   Ibid   263

5   D. Tidball   Builders & Fools   IVP   1999   133

6   Ibid   137

7   Ibid   136

8 C. Seville in The Fire And The Clay Ibid 115

9 F. Wright Pastoral Care For Lay People SCM Press 1982 23

10 C. Seville Ibid 117

11 Ibid 116

12 C. Cocksworth & R. Brown Ibid 33

13 Ibid 33-34

14 Ibid 34

15 D. Tidball Ibid 94

16 Ibid 88

17 Ibid 97

CHAPTER 5

1 C. Cocksworth & R. Brown Ibid 38

2 D. Tidball Ibid 106

3 Ibid 105

4 Ibid 104

5 Ibid 114

6 D. Lonsdale Dance To The Music Of The Spirit: The Art of Discernment
   DLT 1992 27

7   R. Greenway in The Pastor Evangelist Edited by Greenway Presbyterian & Reformed   Pub: 1987   182

8   Ibid   2

9   Ibid   3

10   Ibid   11

11   Brian J. Kallenberg   Live To Tell - Evangelism For A Post Modern Age Brazos Press   2002   13

12   Ibid   32

13   Ibid   38

14   C. Cocksworth & R. Brown Ibid   130

15   New Bible Dictionary   IVP   1982   486

16   Ibid   487

17   Ibid   487

18   C. Cocksworth & R. Brown   Ibid   132

19   Ibid   137

20   Ibid   142

21   Ibid   68-69

22   J. Gledhill   ibid   38

23   Marva Dawn Reaching Out Without Dumbing Down Eerdmans 1995 80

24 Ibid   80

25 Graham Kendrick   Worship   Kingsway   1984   23

26 D. Peterson   Engaging With God – A Biblical Theology Of Worship
    Apollos 1992   17

27 Ibid   19

28 Ibid   46

29 C. Cocksworth & R. Brown   ibid   71

30 R. Barron in Priesthood In The Modern World   Ibid 94 – 95

31 Ibid   98

32 Ibid   96

33 C. Cocksworth & R. Brown   Ibid   71

34 M. Selman   Sacrifice In The Bible Edited R. T & M. J. Selman
    Baker 1995   161 - 162

35 Ibid   162

36 Marva Dawn   A Royal Waste Of Time   Eerdmans   1999   23 – 36

37 I. Bradley   Ibid   109

38 M. Selman   Ibid   158

39 Ibid   158

40 Steve Walton   Sacrifice In The Bible   Ibid   140

41 Ibid   139

42 Ibid   139

43 Raymond Brown   Ibid   61

44 Raymond Brown   Ibid   62

45 N. & C. Henshall in Priests In A People's Church G. Guiver SPCK 2001 90

46 Daniel O. Leary   Year Of The Heart   Paulist Press   1989   85-87

47 Wayne Crudem   The Gift Of Prophecy   Kingsway   1988   17

48 Clifford Hill   Prophecy Past And Present   Highland   1989   13

49 Thomas P. Rausch S. J. in Theology Of Priesthood
    Edited by Goergen & Carrido   The Liturgical Press   2000   106

50 Ibid   106

51 Ibid   107

52 W. Brueggemann   The Prophetic Imagination   Fortress Press   2001 X11

53 Ibid X1V

54 Ibid X

55 Ibid XX

56 Ibid 3

57 Ibid 9

58 K. Leech   Spirituality And Pastoral Care   Ibid   133

59 Steven Glover article in the Daily Mail   21st June 2003

CHAPTER 6

1   ACCM Occasional Paper No 10 1982 - The Training Of Training
    Incumbents (part 1)   1

1   Ibid   1

3   Ibid   4

4   Ibid   5

5   Ibid   5

6   Neil Burgess   Into Deep Water   Kevin Mayhew   1998   15

7   Ibid   26

8   Ibid   28

9   Ibid   132-133

10 ACCM Occasional Paper 10 1982   Ibid   2

11 Ibid   3

12 ABM Ministry Paper No 17   1998   11

13 Ibid   15

14 Neil Burgess   Ibid   31

15 Ibid   32

16 Summary – The Hind Report   Formation for Ministry Within A
    Learning Church   Ministry Division of The Archbishop's Council
    Church House Publishing   2003   1

17 Ibid   2

18 The Hind Report – Formation For Ministry within A Learning Church
    Ministry Division of The Archbishop's Council
    Church House Publishing 2003   139

19 Summary – The Hind Report   Ibid   12

20 The Hind Report   80

21 Ibid   16

22 Ibid   42

23 Ibid   43

24 Ibid   44

25 Ibid   45

26 Ibid   47

27 Ibid   48

28 Ibid   47

29 Ibid   66

30 Ibid   29

31 Ibid   29

32 ABM Policy paper   3A 1993   101

33 Yvonne Warren   The Cracked Pot   Kevin Mayhew   2003   197

34 The Hind Report   Ibid   42

35 Michael Green   Adventure Of Faith   Zondervann   2001   80

36 Ibid   83

37 John Betjeman   Church Poems   Pan Books   1981   71 - 73

38 ABM Ministry paper No 17   January 1998 – Guidelines For
    Ministerial Formation And Personal Development In The First Four
    Years After Ordination   1

39 Ibid   2

40 Ibid   3

41 Ibid   13

42 Ibid   15

APPENDIX1

1 ABM Policy Paper 6: 1995 A Review Of Selection Procedures In the Church of England: The Report of A Working party 3

2 Ibid 25

APPENDIX 2

1 Andrew R. Irvine Between Two Worlds Mowbray 1997 89

2 Ibid 90

3 Ibid 89

4 Ibid 96

5 Ibid 91 – 93

6 J. Kotva Jr. in Practice What You Preach Edited by J. F. Keenan S. J. & J. Kotva Jr. Sheed & Ward 1999 72

7 Ibid 72

8 Ibid 74

9 Ibid 75

10 Ibid 76

11 Alan Abernethy Fulfilment & Frustration Columba Press 2002 118

BIBLIOGRAPHY

Alan Abernethy Fulfilment & Frustration – Ministry In Today's Church Columba Press 2002

Beckwith & Selman Editors Sacrifice In The Bible Paternoster Press 1995

John Betjeman Church Poems Pan Books 1981

Ian Bradley The Power Of Sacrifice D L T 1995

Raymond Brown Hebrews IVP 1982

F. D. Bruner A Theology Of The Holy Spirit Eerdmans 1974

Neil Burgess Into Deep Water Kevin Mayhew 1998

Walter Brueggemann The Prophetic Imagination Fortress Press 2001

C. Cocksworth & R. Brown Being A Priest Today Canterbury Press 2002

Sean Connolly Simple Priesthood Paulist Press 2001

Steven Croft Ministry In Three Dimensions D L T 2000

Wayne Crudem The Gift Of Prophecy Kingsway 1988

D. Dales Glory - The Spiritual Theology Of Michael Ramsay Canterbury Press 2003

M. Fallon A Priest After My Own Heart St. Paul's 2001

Jonathan Gledhill Leading A Local Church SPCK 2003

Goergen & Garrido Editors The Theology Of Priesthood Liturgical Press 2000

Michael Green   Adventure Of Faith   Zondervaan   2001

R. Greenway The Pastor Evangelist Presbyterian & Reformed Publisher 1987

R. Greenwood   Transforming Church   SPCK   2002

R. Greenwood   Transforming Priesthood   SPCK   1999

G. Guiver et al   The Fire And The Clay: The Priest In Today's Church   SPCK   1999

G. Guiver   Priests In A People's Church   SPCK   2001

Scott Hahn   The Lamb's Supper   DLT   1999

George Herbert   Selected Poems   Everyman   1996

Clifford Hill   Prophecy Past And Present   Highland   1989

The Hind Report Ministry Division Of The Archbishop's Council Church House Publishing   2003

The Hind Report - Summary   Ministry Division Of The Archbishop's Council   Church House Publishing   2003

Andrew R. Irvine   Between Two Worlds   Mowbray   1997

B. J. Kallenberg   Live To Tell - Evangelism In A Post Modern Age   Brazos Press   2002

J. F. Keenan S. J. & Kotva Jr. Editors   Practice What You Preach   Sheed & Ward   1999

Kenneth Leech   Soul Friend   DLT   1996

Kenneth Leech   Spirituality And Pastoral Care   Sheldon Press 1986

David Lonsdale   Dance To The Music Of The Spirit: The Art
Of Discernment   DLT   1992

Kenneth Mason   Priesthood In Society   Canterbury Press   2002

Arthur Middleton   Towards A Renewed Priesthood
Gracewing   1995

R. C. Moberly   Ministerial Priesthood   John Murray
London   1899

Watchman Nee   The Normal Christian Life   Kingsway   1989

New Bible Dictionary   IVP   1984

Julian of Norwich   Showing of Love   Translated by Julia
Bolton Holloway   DLT   2003

D. J. O'Leary   The Year Of The Heart   Paulist Press 1989

Michael Perham   New Handbook Of Pastoral Liturgy   SPCK
2002

Michael Ramsay   The Christian Priest Today   SPCK   1987

Tom Smail   The Giving Gift   DLT   1994

K. S. Smith   Editor   Priesthood In The Modern World   Sheed
& Ward   1999

Charles Stanley   The Wonderful Spirit Filled Life   Nelson   1992

Kenneth Stevenson   Do This – The Shape, Style and Meaning
Of The Eucharist Canterbury Press   2002

Derek Tidball   Builders And Fools   IVP   1999

T. F. Torrance   A Royal Priesthood – A Theology Of The
Ordained Ministry   T & T Clark   1999

John Twistleton   Empowering Priesthood   Tufton Books   2002

Evelyn Underhill   The Ways Of The Spirit   Crossroad   1992

Miroslav Volf   Exclusion And Embrace   Abingdon Press   1996

Yvonne Warren   The Cracked Pot   Kevin Mayhew   2003

Gordon Wenham   Leviticus   Eerdmans   1979

Frank Wright   Pastoral Care For Lay People   SCM Press   1982

ACCM Occasional Paper 10: The Training Of Training Incumbents   September 1982

ACCM Occasional Paper 12: Selection For Ministry – A Report On The Criteria June 1983 (revised August 1990)

ACCM 22: Education For The Church's Ministry   1987

ABM Policy Paper 3A: The Report Of A Working Party On Criteria For Selection For Ministry In the Church of England October 1993

ABM Policy Paper 6:   A Review Of Selection Procedures In the Church of England: The Report of A Working Party September 1995

ABM Ministry Paper 17: Beginning Public Ministry – Guidelines For Ministerial Formation And Personal Development For The First Four Years Of Ministry   January 1998

Going To A Selection Conference   The Ministry Division The Archbishop's Council   1999